PERCEIVING:
A Philosophical Study

BY RODERICK M. CHISHOLM

Professor of Philosophy, Brown University

Cornell University Press
Ithaca, New York

*This work has been brought to publication with
the assistance of a grant from the Ford Foundation.*

© 1957 by Cornell University

Cornell University Press

First published 1957
Second printing 1961
Third printing 1963
Fourth printing 1966
Fifth printing 1968

T 1603259625

PRINTED IN THE UNITED STATES OF AMERICA
BY VALLEY OFFSET, INC.
BOUND BY VAIL-BALLOU PRESS, INC.

Preface

THIS book is about some of the philosophical puzzles or problems that arise when we think and talk about perceiving. I propose ways of dealing with these puzzles or problems; I attempt either to solve them or to correct what seem to me to be the mistakes which give rise to them. The book is not polemical; I did not set out with the intention of defending any particular philosophical theses or techniques. Some of the views of other philosophers are discussed, but only to throw light upon what I have wanted to say.

Many but not all of the puzzles or problems discussed here arise because of our failure to understand the interrelations among the words we use when we talk about perceiving. There are two methods of dealing with such puzzles or problems. We might examine in detail the ways in which people talk about perceiving and then try to show that our philosophical questions arise because of our failure to use our own language consistently or unambiguously. Or we might propose ways of

Preface

talking about perceiving, ways of talking that are adequate to what we know or want to be able to say about perceiving, and then try to show that, by restricting ourselves to these ways of talking, we avoid the philosophical questions to which the use of ordinary locutions seems to give rise. I have used both of these methods but have relied somewhat more upon the second.

If we are to express all we know about perceiving, we must give certain words a use which no words need to have when we are merely expressing the conclusions of physics and the natural sciences. Most of the philosophical questions about perceiving are usually formulated in these "nonphysicalistic" words and locutions; I have tried, therefore, to use as few of them as possible. I have formulated a number of definitions in order to show that many of these terms can be avoided and that, when they are avoided, some of our philosophical puzzles and problems can be satisfactorily handled. But I believe that, if we are to discuss perceiving adequately, we need at least three types of expression which are not needed in physics and the natural sciences.

Avoid physicalistic words & locutions

First, we must use an *epistemic* locution—a locution enabling us to say what we often say using such words as "know," "evident," "unreasonable," "perceive," "see," and "probable." Secondly, we must use some locution to perform one of the many functions for which we ordinarily use the word "appear." And thirdly, we must use an "intentional" term, a term that will perform one of the functions for which we ordinarily use the word "believe." There are, I suggest, still other "nonphysicalistic" terms we must use if we are to express all we know about psychology; but I do not here discuss these terms and, so far as possible, I try to avoid using them.

The first part of the book—"The Ethics of Belief"—is concerned with what is expressed by such words as "know," "perceive," and "evident" when they are used epistemically. In

Preface

Chapter One, I propose definitions of such words, using one undefined epistemic locution. This is a locution enabling us to say that some propositions are more worthy of belief than are others. In Chapter Two, I discuss the relations between our epistemic vocabulary and the technical terms of the theory of probability and the logic of confirmation. And in Chapter Three, I attempt to formulate "the problem of the criterion"—a problem having to do with the *application* of our epistemic vocabulary.

Using some of our epistemic terms—for example, "know," "perceive," or "evident"—we can readily describe the conditions under which others may be applied. Using our epistemic vocabulary, we can describe conditions which are such that, for any hypothesis or proposition, if these conditions obtain then someone has *adequate evidence* for that hypothesis or proposition, or *knows* or *perceives* it to be true. But can we describe such conditions *without* using any epistemic terms? I shall attempt to do this in the second part of the book ("Evidence"). It is by reference to this question, which has its analogue in moral philosophy, that we can best understand what philosophers have said about knowledge and evidence. "Empiricism," in one of the traditional senses of this term, refers to a possible answer, but it is an answer I shall reject.

Chapter Seven—"Knowing about Evidence"—concerns a very difficult question concerning the "objectivity" of our epistemic judgments, our judgments about knowledge and evidence. This question, too, has its analogue in moral philosophy.

The third part of the book—"The Objects of Perception"— is concerned with questions of a somewhat different kind. I shall discuss the nonepistemic use of perception words ("He *saw* his brother but didn't realize who it was") and its relation to the epistemic use of these words ("He saw *that* it was his brother"); and I shall consider the relations between perceiving,

Preface

in these two senses, and "being appeared to." It will then be possible to show, I think, that some of the more paradoxical statements that philosophers and scientists have made about perceiving rest upon obvious errors.

In defining the epistemic use of perception words, it seems to be necessary to make use of the term "believe," or "assume." In the final chapter, I shall consider some of the attempts to define this use of "believe," or "assume," behavioristically. I suggest that these attempts have so far been unsuccessful. This fact, I shall argue, lends some presumption to the view which has been expressed by saying that "intentional inexistence" is peculiar to psychological phenomena.

I am dissatisfied with some of the conclusions I have advocated, and I know that the book leaves us with a number of new problems. But my various conclusions hang together in a way which may not be immediately apparent; it is likely that revision of any one of them will make it necessary to revise many of the others. And no other combination of solutions seems to me as plausible as the one I propose.

Much of Parts I and II was presented in lecture form in February and March, 1956, at King's College and University College, in London, at the University of Birmingham, and at the University of Graz. I wish to thank the editors of the following journals who have permitted me to use parts of articles first appearing in their journals: *Journal of Philosophy* (for parts of Chapter Two and the Appendix), *Philosophical Studies* (for parts of Chapter Eleven), *Philosophy and Phenomenological Research* (for parts of Chapters One and Eight), and *Revue Internationale de Philosophie* (for parts of Chapter Ten). I wish also to express my thanks to the editor of *Analysis*, to Harcourt, Brace and Company, to Robert M. McBride and Company, and to Charles Scribner's Sons for permitting quota-

Preface

tions from the following works: Moritz Schlick, "Facts and Propositions," *Analysis*, II (1935), 70; Leon Chwistek, *The Limits of Science*, pp. 288–289; H. H. Price, *Perception*, p. 185; and C. I. Lewis, *Mind and the World-Order*, pp. 122–123.

This book was made possible by a generous grant given to me by the Howard Foundation while I was on leave from Brown University during the academic year 1955–1956. I am also indebted to Professors John Ladd, Wesley Salmon, and Richard Taylor, for criticism of parts of early versions of the manuscript; to Professors C. A. Baylis, Austin Duncan-Jones, John W. Lenz, and Vincent A. Tomas and the late Professor R. M. Blake, with whom I have discussed many of the matters taken up here; to Mr. Timothy Duggan, who has read and criticized many versions of this book; and to Professors C. I. Lewis and Donald Williams, my former teachers. I wish finally to record my special indebtedness to my teacher and colleague, Professor C. J. Ducasse, to my wife, and to my mother.

RODERICK M. CHISHOLM

Brown University
January 1957

Contents

xi

PART I

The Ethics of Belief

One

Epistemic Terms

1. If a man looks toward the roof and *sees* that his cat is there, he is not likely to *say*, "I have adequate evidence for the proposition or hypothesis that that is a cat," "I take that to be a cat," or "There is something which is appearing to me in a certain way." But, I suggest, if he does see that his cat is there, then he has adequate evidence for the proposition that a cat is there; moreover, there is something—his cat—which he *takes* to be his cat and which *is* appearing to him in a certain way. And I would suggest, more generally, that the locution "S perceives something to have such and such a characteristic," in one of its most important uses, may be defined as follows:

(1) "There is something that S *perceives* to be *f*" means: there is an *x* which is *f* and which appears in some way to S; S takes *x* to be *f*; and S has adequate evidence for the proposition that *x* is *f*.

By adding qualifications about sense organs, we could formulate similar definitions of important uses of "see" and of "hear."

Such definitions are not interesting or significant unless we can say what is meant by "appear," "take," and "adequate evidence" without using "see," "hear," or "perceive." I will begin, then, with "adequate evidence." In trying to understand this term, we will find ourselves involved in a number of philosophical problems.

2. "Adequate evidence"—like "acceptable," "unreasonable," "indifferent," "certain," "probable," and "improbable"—is a term we use in appraising the epistemic, or cognitive, worth of propositions, hypotheses, and beliefs. The statements in which we express such appraisal—for example, "We do not have adequate evidence for believing that acquired characteristics are inherited," "The astronomy of Ptolemy is unreasonable," and "In all probability, the accused is innocent"—are similar in significant respects to "Stealing is wicked," "We ought to forgive our enemies," and other statements expressing our ethical or moral appraisals. Many of the characteristics which philosophers and others have thought peculiar to ethical statements also hold of epistemic statements. And when we consider the application of "evident" and our other epistemic terms, we meet with problems very much like those traditionally associated with "right," "good," and "duty."

I shall propose definitions of several important epistemic terms. The definitions are intended to be adequate only to some of the epistemic uses of the terms defined. Many of the terms I shall define have other, nonepistemic uses I shall not mention. And there are many terms having important epistemic uses which I shall not attempt to define; the epistemic uses of such terms, I believe, can be defined by means of the epistemic vocabulary presented here. The definitions make use of one undefined epistemic locution. This is the locution: "h is more worthy of S's belief than i," where "S" may be replaced by the name of a person and "*h*" and "*i*" by names of propositions, statements, or hypotheses. An alternative reading is "*h* is more acceptable than *i* for S." In subsequent chapters I shall discuss the application of our epistemic vocabulary, and in Chapter Seven I shall discuss the meaning of our undefined locution.

3. A proposition, statement, or hypothesis is <u>unreasonable</u> if it is less worthy of belief than is its denial or contradictory. Let us say, then:

> (2) "It would be *unreasonable* for S to accept *h*" means that non-*h* is more worthy of S's belief than *h*.

If S *does* accept *h*, we may say, of course, that it *is* unreasonable of him to do so. When it is clear from the general context what subject S is intended, we may say, elliptically, that a proposition, statement, or hypothesis is unreasonable.

"Absurd" and "preposterous" are sometimes synonyms of "unreasonable" in its present sense. And the belief—or feeling —that a proposition is unreasonable may also be expressed by means of imperatives. If I say to you, "Don't count on seeing me before Thursday," I may mean that it would be unreasonable of you to believe that you will see me before Thursday.

Whenever it would be unreasonable for a man to accept a certain proposition, then he may be said to have *adequate evidence* for its contradictory. Our next definition is:

> (3) "S has *adequate evidence* for *h*" means that it would be unreasonable for S to accept non-*h*.

When it is clear what subject S is intended, then we may speak elliptically, once again, and say that a proposition, statement, or hypothesis is *evident*. The expression "adequate evidence" as it is used in this definition should be thought of as a single term; I use it because it seems to be ordinarily used in such contexts. An alternative locution which I shall also use is "*h* is evident for S."

As examples of propositions which are evident, we could cite what a man knows or perceives to be true. But we are not defining "adequate evidence" in terms "know" or "perceive." In definition (1) we have defined "perceive" in terms of "adequate evidence." And in definition (6) we shall define "know" in terms of "adequate evidence." There are, moreover, propositions for which a man may have adequate evidence without knowing or perceiving them to be true. For there are times when, as we would ordinarily say, the available evidence may favor some proposition which is false; at such times, a false proposition is more worthy of one's belief than is a true proposition. Thus it may be true that a man is going to win a lottery and yet unreasonable for him to believe that he is. But once the drawings are announced, the belief may no longer be unreasonable.

The example indicates that our definitions should contain temporal references. For a proposition may be evident at one date and unreasonable at another. The phrase "at *t*" could be inserted in our definitions: a proposition would then be said to be evident *at a time t* provided only that its contradictory is unreasonable at *t*; and so on. But, for simplicity, I shall not make these temporal references explicit.

The *evident*, according to our definition, is more worthy of belief than is the unreasonable. But there is another sense of the phrase "worthy of belief" in which we can say, more simply, that the *true* is more worthy of belief than the false. If the evident, as I have suggested, is sometimes false, then there are hypotheses which, in the one sense, are more worthy of belief than are their contradictories but which, in the other, are less. This twofold sense of "worthy" is not peculiar to our epistemic

6

terms, but holds of ethical terms generally. Following Richard Price, let us distinguish between the *absolute* and the *practical* senses of these terms.[1]

Using the ethical term "right" in its *absolute* sense, we may say that no one can ever know what actions are right; for no one can ever know what *all* of the consequences of any action will be. In this absolute sense of "right," perhaps it would have been right for someone to have killed Hitler and Stalin when they were infants; perhaps their parents acted (absolutely) wrongly in allowing them to live.[2] But in the *practical* sense of "right" such killings would *not* have been right. It was not possible, when Hitler and Stalin were infants, for anyone to foresee the harm they would do and, I think we may assume, there is no motive which would have justified putting them to death. If we try, as some philosophers do, to restrict "right" and "wrong" and other ethical terms to their absolute use, then other terms must take over their practical use. We might then say of the killings we have been discussing that, although they might have been right, they would hardly have been *praiseworthy*—or that, although they would not have been wrong, they would certainly have been *blameworthy*.

We cannot know, of any action, whether it is right or wrong in the absolute senses of these terms unless we know what all of its consequences are going to be. But, I believe, we can know, of any contemplated act of our own, whether it is right or wrong in the practical senses of these terms; we can know of any act we contemplate whether that act would be praiseworthy or blameworthy.

[1] See Richard Price, *Review of the Principal Questions of Morals* (Oxford, 1948; first published in 1787), ch. viii. Compare H. A. Prichard's "Duty and Ignorance of Fact," reprinted in his *Moral Obligation* (Oxford, 1950), and W. D. Ross, *Foundations of Ethics* (London, 1939), ch. vii.

[2] Compare Bertrand Russell, *Human Knowledge* (New York, 1948), pt. v, ch. vi.

7

When it is said, then, that people ought to believe what is evident and that they ought not to believe what is unreasonable, "ought" has its practical use. But when it is said that they ought to believe what is true and that they ought not to believe what is false, "ought" has its absolute use.[3] Our locution "*h* is more worthy of belief than *i*" is to be taken in its practical sense. And all of the other epistemic terms to be used here are, similarly, to be taken in a practical and not in an absolute sense.

I shall return to this distinction in Chapter Three.

4. Let us say that a proposition, statement, or hypothesis is acceptable provided only that it is not unreasonable.

(4) "*h* is *acceptable* for S" means: it is false that it would be unreasonable for S to accept *h*.

In other words, if the contradictory of a proposition is not evident, then the proposition is acceptable. "Justifiable," "reasonable," or "credible" might be used in place of "acceptable" here; I have avoided them, however, because in their ordinary use in such contexts they are often taken as synonymous with "evident." The modal term "*possible*" is sometimes used as a synonym of "acceptable"; when a man says, "It is possible that we will have good news tomorrow," he may mean it is not unreasonable of us to believe that we will have good news tomorrow.

---

[3] There is a useful discussion of this distinction in R. B. Braithwaite, *Scientific Explanation* (Cambridge, 1953), pp. 279 ff. In *The Origin of the Knowledge of Right and Wrong* (London, 1902), sec. 23, Franz Brentano says in effect that we ought to believe only what is true. In a colloquium entitled "The Normative in the Descriptive," Konstantin Kolenda and Abraham Edel say we ought to believe only what is true, while Alan Ross Anderson, Max Black, and Irving Copi say there are times when we need not believe what is true (*Review of Metaphysics*, X [1956], 106–121).

Epistemic Terms

In his lecture "The Ethics of Belief," W. K. Clifford said, "It is wrong to believe upon insufficient evidence." [4] His ethics was somewhat more rigid than that suggested here, for he held that, for each of us, there is a large class of propositions concerning which we ought to withhold both assent and denial. But I have suggested, in effect, that a proposition should be treated as innocent until proven guilty. It is only when we have adequate evidence for the contradictory of a proposition that it is unreasonable for us to accept the proposition. We have adequate evidence for the proposition that Eisenhower was President in 1956; hence it is unreasonable for us to accept the proposition that he was *not* President in 1956. We do not now have adequate evidence for the proposition that a Republican will be President in 1975; Clifford would say, therefore, that we ought not to believe that a Republican will be President in 1975. I suggest that we *may* believe this, that the proposition is "acceptable" in the sense defined above. [5] But to say that we have a right to believe it is not to say that we have a right to bet our savings on it.

We may say that a hypothesis is acceptable for someone without implying that it is always reasonable for him to *act upon* it; indeed, we may say that he has *adequate evidence* for a hypothesis without implying that it is always reasonable for him to act upon it. And in saying that in a certain instance it may be reasonable for a man to act upon a hypothesis, we

---

[4] W. K. Clifford, *Lectures and Essays*, vol. II (London, 1879). It should be noted that our definitions, as they now stand, have this limitation: they do not enable us to formulate Clifford's position, for we cannot consistently say that a hypothesis and its contradictory are *both* unreasonable.

[5] Compare this dialogue from Sheridan's *The Rivals*: "Absolute: 'Sure, Sir, this is not very reasonable, to summon my affection for a lady I know nothing of.' Sir Anthony: 'I am sure, Sir, 'tis more unreasonable in you to object to a lady you know nothing of'" (quoted by J. M. Keynes in *A Treatise on Probability* [London, 1921], p. 41).

9

do not imply that the hypothesis is one for which he has adequate evidence. A man may have adequate evidence for believing he will win if he plays Russian roulette; he may also have adequate evidence for believing he will be paid $10 if he does win. But it would be foolish of him to play, despite the fact that, in so doing, he would be acting upon hypotheses for which he has adequate evidence. On the other hand, a swimmer may have adequate evidence for the hypothesis that he cannot swim ashore and yet be in a position wherein it would be unreasonable of him *not* to act upon it. And often, when we take precautionary measures—when we buy insurance, for example—we are justified in acting on hypotheses which are unreasonable and which we believe to be false. In deciding whether to act upon a hypothesis we must consider, not only the evidence that bears upon the hypothesis itself, but also the evidence that bears upon the "utility" or "moral gain" of acting upon it. We should try to decide, for example, what the value of acting upon the hypothesis would be if the hypothesis were true, what the "disvalue" of acting upon the hypothesis would be if the hypothesis were false, and we must try to compare these values and disvalues.[6] And we should also consider whether we ought to inquire further— whether we ought to seek out *additional* evidence. I have adequate evidence for the hypothesis that this is a piece of paper and in setting out to write I may be satisfied with the evidence at hand; but before betting my savings on the hypothesis I should make a more thorough investigation.

The question whether to *accept* a certain hypothesis— whether to *believe* it—is thus easier to answer than the ques-

---

[6] These concepts are discussed with more exactness in writings on probability. See, for example, Rudolf Carnap, *Logical Foundations of Probability* (Chicago, 1950), pp. 226–279.

tion of whether to *act upon* it.[7] In deciding whether to accept it, we need not consider the "utility" or "moral gain"
that would result from acting upon it. And we need not consider whether we ought to make further inquiry and investigation.

If a proposition, statement, or hypothesis is acceptable but
not evident, then its contradictory is also acceptable but not
evident. Such a proposition might be called epistemically indifferent. We may add, then, the following definition:

(5) "*h* is *indifferent* for S" means: (i) it is false that S has
adequate evidence for *h* and (ii) it is also false that S
has adequate evidence for non-*h*.

The hypothesis that it will rain in London a year from today
is, for most of us, epistemically indifferent; we do not have
adequate evidence either for it or for its contradictory. If a
proposition or hypothesis is indifferent, its contradictory is also
indifferent. An indifferent proposition is thus one which is
neither evident nor unreasonable. According to Clifford, no
proposition is epistemically indifferent. According to the "absolute skeptic," all propositions are epistemically indifferent.[8]

If we were to need the term "dubitable," meaning fit to
be disbelieved, we could define "*h* is *dubitable* for S" as
"non-*h* is acceptable for S." We could then say that an epi-

---

[7] I suggest that the concept of *acting upon* a hypothesis must be defined
by reference to *action, purpose,* and *belief* in some such way as this. "In
acting A, S is *acting upon h*" means: in acting A, S is trying to produce
E; and he is acting as he would act if, further, (i) he believed *h* and (ii)
he believed that A will result in E if and only if *h* is true. I shall not
discuss the concepts of *purpose* and *action* in this book.

[8] See Sextus Empiricus, *Outlines of Pyrrhonism*, bk. I, especially pp. 9,
112, and 123 of vol. I of *Sextus Empiricus* (Loeb Classical Library, London,
1933).

stemically indifferent proposition is one that is both acceptable and dubitable.

5. Without attempting to formulate an exact logic of epistemic terms, let us note certain <u>principles which have been assumed in the foregoing.</u> The expressions "*h* is more worthy of S's belief than non-*h*" and "non-*h* is more worthy of S's belief than *h*" are contraries; they may both be false but they cannot both be true. (We should suppose that these expressions contain the temporal reference "at *t*.") Hence, for any hypothesis *h* and any subject S, either *h* is acceptable for S or non-*h* is acceptable for S. This principle is not incompatible with saying that some hypotheses are epistemically indifferent; for, although it says, of any hypothesis and its contradictory, that at least one is acceptable, it does not preclude the possibility of both being acceptable.

In an important series of studies, G. H. von Wright has pointed out the logical analogy which holds between the *ethical* terms "wrong," "obligatory," "permitted," and "indifferent," respectively, and the *modal* terms "impossible," "necessary," "possible," and "contingent." [9] The analogy also holds between each of these sets of terms and our *epistemic* terms "unreasonable," "evident," "acceptable," and "indifferent." ("Dubitable" would correspond to the terms "unrequired" and

---

[9] Compare G. H. von Wright, *An Essay in Modal Logic* (Amsterdam, 1951); "Deontic Logic," *Mind*, LX (1951), 1–13; and "On the Logic of Some Axiological and Epistemological Concepts," *Ajatus* (Helsinki), XVII (1952), 213–234. Although Von Wright does not discuss the epistemic concepts listed above, much of what I have said about the first four concepts is suggested by his work. In the *Ajatus* article, he introduces the epistemological concepts "falsified," "verified," "not-falsified," and "undecided." Compare Alan Ross Anderson, *The Formal Analysis of Normative Systems* (Technical Report no. 2, Interaction Laboratory, Sociology Department, Yale University, 1956).

"unnecessary.") The assumptions discussed below have their analogues in ethics and in modal logic.

We should assume that the conjunction "*h* is acceptable for S and *i* is acceptable for S" does *not* imply "The conjunction of *h* and *i* is acceptable for S." The hypothesis that a certain object is a dog may be acceptable; the hypothesis that it is a stone may also be acceptable; but the hypothesis that it is both a dog and a stone is unreasonable. On the other hand, the conjunction "*h* is evident for S and *i* is evident for S" is equivalent to "The conjunction, *h* and *i*, is evident for S." If it is evident that the thief worked alone and also evident that he came at night, then it is evident that he worked alone and came at night. We should assume, further, that the disjunction "Either *h* is acceptable for S or *i* is acceptable for S" is equivalent to "The disjunction, *h* or *i*, is acceptable for S." But "The disjunction, *h* or *i*, is *evident* for S" is *not* equivalent to "Either *h* is evident for S or *i* is evident for S." It is now evident, for example, that the next man to be elected President of the United States will be either a Democrat or a Republican, but it is not now evident that he will be a Democrat and it is not now evident that he will be a Republican.

Note that we may form a logical square, whose upper right and left corners are, respectively, "evident" and "unreasonable," and whose lower right and left corners are "acceptable" and "dubitable." For "*h* is evident" implies "*h* is acceptable" and contradicts "*h* is dubitable," and "*h* is unreasonable" implies "*h* is dubitable" and contradicts "*h* is acceptable."

I have been assuming that, if it is unreasonable for S to accept *h*, then S ought to *refrain* from accepting *h*. If we wish to avoid a rigid ethics of belief, we may confine our principles to what one ought to *refrain* from believing. In such a case, we may say that a man fulfills his epistemic obligations provided only that he doesn't believe what he ought not to believe. A more rigid ethics would be concerned, more positively, with what we *ought* to believe. It might tell us, for example, that, if a proposition is unreasonable and therefore one which ought *not* to be accepted, then its contradictory, which is evident, is a proposition which *ought* to be accepted. For our present purposes, it is not necessary to make a decision concerning these two types of ethics.[10]

An adequate epistemology would also include such principles as this: if it is evident that *h* implies *i* and if *i* is unreasonable, then *h* is unreasonable. It may be evident, for example, that if the Senator votes, he will vote against his party. If it is unreasonable to believe that he will vote against his party, then it is also unreasonable to believe that he will vote. But if, on the other hand, the hypothesis that he will vote is acceptable, then so, too, is the hypothesis that he will vote against his party.

There are other epistemic principles whose status is more difficult to determine. Suppose, for example, that *h* is evident, that *h* entails *i*, but that it is not evident that *h* entails *i*. Should we say, in such a case, that *i* is evident? R. B. Braithwaite, in *Scientific Explanation*, discusses similar questions in some detail, noting that the issues which they involve are very much like those involved in distinguishing between what we have called the "practical" and "absolute" senses of the ethical terms "right" and "duty." [11]

---

[10] Some ought-statements—for example, "If you want to be happy, you ought to believe in God"—are concerned only with telling how to bring about certain ends, ends which can be described without ethical or epistemic terms. But ought-statements in contexts such as the above should not be interpreted in this way; I shall consider their interpretation in Chapter Seven.

[11] R. B. Braithwaite, *Scientific Explanation*, pp. 279 ff. Compare C. S. Peirce, *Collected Papers* (Cambridge, Mass., 1931), I, 311 ff.; C. I. Lewis, "Right Believing and Concluding," in *The Ground and Nature of the Right* (New York, 1955), ch. ii; and G. Polya, *Patterns of Plausible Inference* (Princeton, 1954), *passim*.

6. Let us now consider the epistemic uses of "know"—its uses in such statements as "He knows the earth to be round" and "The speaker knows that the hall is filled."

A number of authors have tried to reduce this epistemic sense of know—*knowing that*—to a kind of verbal *knowing how.* "Knowing that some fact is the case is to know how to tell the truth about matters of a certain kind." [12] Knowing that the earth is round, according to this conception, differs from knowing how to swim only in that a different kind of skill or aptness is involved, namely, "the capacity to state correctly what is the case." [13] If, by "the capacity to state correctly what is the case," we were to mean merely "the capacity to utter words truly describing what is the case," then this capacity, like the ability to swim, *would* be a kind of aptness of the body. But if we define "knowing that the earth is round" in terms of *this* capacity—the capacity to utter the sentence "The earth is round" (or some other sentence having the same meaning)—then we must say, of most of those people who believe that the earth is *flat*, that they *know* that it is round. For most of those people are capable of uttering the sentence "The earth is round." Hence a qualification must be introduced in the phrase "the capacity of uttering words truly describing what is the case" if this phrase is to provide us with an adequate definition of *knowing that.*[14]

A definition of *knowing that* should be adequate, moreover, to the distinction between *knowing* and *believing truly.* If I now predict the winner on the basis of what the tea leaves

---

[12] John Watling, "Inferences from the Known to the Unknown," *Proceedings of the Aristotelian Society*, LV (1954–1955), 58.

[13] John Hartland-Swann, "The Logical Status of 'Knowing That,'" *Analysis*, XVI (1956), 114.

[14] Still other complications which this "verbal aptitude" definition of *knowing that* involves are discussed in Chapter Eleven, Section 3.

say, then, even though my prediction may be true, I cannot now be said to *know* that it is true.

"Knowing that," I suggest, has at least two epistemic senses. In what follows, I shall confine "know" to the broader of these senses and use "certain" for the narrower sense. The following, then, will be our definition of "know":

> (6) "S *knows* that *h* is true" means: (i) S accepts *h*; (ii) S has adequate evidence for *h*; and (iii) *h* is true.

If we wish to avoid the term "true," we may substitute this formulation:

> "S knows that . . ." means: (i) S accepts the hypothesis (or proposition) that . . . ; (ii) S has adequate evidence for the hypothesis (or proposition) that . . . ; and (iii). . . .

Or we may use the locution of definition (1) and speak of S knowing "that *x* is *f*."

The term "accepts" which appears in (6) has not been previously defined; I shall discuss it in detail in Chapter Eleven. "Assumes" is an alternative: for "S accepts *h*" is replaceable by "S assumes that *h* is true"; and "S accepts the proposition or hypothesis that *x* is *f*" is replaceable by "S assumes that *x* is *f*."

If a man knows, say, that the hall has been painted, then, according to our definition, he accepts the hypothesis that it has been painted, he has adequate evidence for this hypothesis, and, finally, the hall *has* been painted. On the other hand, if he accepts the hypothesis, has adequate evidence for it, but does not *know* that it is true, then the hall has not been painted.

Should we say that, if S knows *h* to be true, then S *believes* that *h* is true? (It should be noted that *believing* a proposition is not the same as asserting, proclaiming, or announcing that one believes it. When we *assert* a proposition and when we *say* that we believe it, then, unless we are lying, we are *acting upon* the proposition. I shall return to this distinction in Chapter Eleven.) There is a sense of "believe," in its ordinary use, which is such that "S believes that *h* is true" entails "S does *not* know that *h* is true." If I *know* that La Paz is in Bolivia, I'm not likely to say, "I believe that La Paz is in Bolivia," for "I *believe* that La Paz is in Bolivia" suggests I don't know that it is. In this use, "S believes that *h* is true" means that S accepts *h* but does not know that *h* is true. Hence, if we interpret "believe" in this way, we cannot say that *knowing* entails *believing*. There is still another use of "believe" which is such that the expression "I believe"—an expression in the first person—entails "I know," or at least entails "I have adequate evidence." If a man says, "His policy, I believe, will not succeed," the parenthetical expression may be intended to express the claim to know or the claim to have adequate evidence that the policy will not succeed.[15]

But "believe" is also used to mean the same as "accept," in the sense in which "accept" is meant above, and in this use *knowing* does entail *believing*. I may believe that *x* is *f*, in this third sense of "believe," and yet not *say*, "I believe that *x* is *f*"; for, as we have noted, when "I believe" is used in this construction (in contrast with its parenthetical use) it is ordinarily intended to express doubt or hesitation. *You* may say of me, however, "He believes that *x* is *f* and, for all I know, he *knows* that *x* is *f*."

But even if there is a sense of "believe," or "accept," in which *knowing* entails *believing*, or *accepting*, we must not think of knowing as being, in any sense, a "species of" be-

---

[15] Compare J. O. Urmson, "Parenthetical Verbs," *Mind*, vol. LXI (1952), reprinted in Antony Flew, ed., *Essays in Conceptual Analysis* (London, 1956).

lieving, or accepting. A man can be said to believe firmly, or reluctantly, or hesitatingly, but no one can be said to *know* firmly, or reluctantly, or hesitatingly. Professor Austin has noted that, although we may ask, "*How* do you know?" and "*Why* do you believe?" we may not ask, "*Why* do you know?" or "*How* do you believe?" [16] The relation of knowing to believing, in the present sense of "believe," is not that of falcon to bird or of airedale to dog; it is more like that of arriving to traveling. *Arriving* entails *traveling*—a man cannot arrive unless he has traveled—but arriving is not a species of traveling.[17]

When we exhort people epistemically, we say, not "You ought to *believe h*," but "You ought to *know h*." If I say to my friend, "You ought to know *h*," it is likely that I accept *h* and believe that he has adequate evidence for *h*; hence the only additional condition I'm exhorting him to meet is that of believing *h*. Or it may be that I claim to know *h* myself and am suggesting that he ought to make further inquiry or investigation (see Section 4 of the present chapter) and that when he does he will then have adequate evidence for *h*. Similar remarks hold of such statements as "You ought to have *known h*."

A second sense of "know" may be obtained by stipulating that the subject *know*, in the first sense, that he has adequate evidence. The statement "S knows that he has adequate evidence" raises important philosophical questions, comparable to certain controversial questions about ethics, which I shall consider in Chapter Seven. If, as many philosophers believe, there is reason to say that people cannot *know* what they ought

---

[16] J. L. Austin, "Other Minds," *Proceedings of the Aristotelian Society*, suppl. vol. XX (1946), reprinted in Antony Flew, ed., *Logic and Language*, 2d ser. (Oxford, 1953).

[17] Professor Gilbert Ryle has used this example in another connection, which I discuss in Chapter Ten, Section 7.

to do, then there is also reason to say that people cannot know which of their beliefs are evident.

Still another sense of "know" may be obtained by stipulating that (ii), in definition (6), describe a *causal* condition of (i). Using "know" in this sense, we cannot say that a man knows a proposition to be true unless we can also say that he believes it *because* he has adequate evidence for it.[18]

7. The term "certain," like "know," is used in many ways. Sometimes it is a synonym for the modal term "necessary"; sometimes one is said to be certain of a proposition only if one is unable to doubt it or if one accepts it with a "maximum degree of confidence"; and sometimes one is said to be certain only if one *knows* that one knows. But the sense of "certain" which is of most importance epistemically, I think, is this:

(7) "S is *certain* that *h* is true" means: (i) S knows that *h* is true and (ii) there is no hypothesis *i* such that *i* is more worthy of S's belief than *h*.

We could avoid "true," if we chose, in the manner suggested in connection with the definition of "know" above.

Sometimes the locution "S is certain" is used to mean merely that S *feels sure*. And in this use, of course, "S is certain" does not imply that S knows. I felt sure that my candidate would win the election, but since he did not, I could not have known that he would.

The present epistemic concept of *certainty* may be illustrated by a quotation from Moritz Schlick. He does not use our epistemic terms, but he is telling us, in effect, that, although statements made by scientists may be evident, they are not cer-

---

[18] In Chapter Six I shall discuss what is sometimes called—misleadingly, I think—"knowledge by acquaintance."

tain and that there are other statements which, in contrast with those of the scientists are certain.

I do have trust in those good fellows, but that is only because I have always found them to be trustworthy whenever I was able to test their enunciations. I assure you most emphatically that I should *not* call the system of science true if I found its consequences incompatible with my own observations of nature, and the fact that it is adopted by the whole of mankind and taught in all the universities would make no impression on me. If all the scientists in the world told me that under certain experimental conditions I must see three black spots, and if under those conditions I saw only one spot, no power in the universe could induce me to think that the statement "there is now only one black spot in the field of vision" is false.[19]

This passage might be interpreted as saying that, at the present moment, there is no hypothesis, not even the best-confirmed hypotheses of science, which is more acceptable than the hypothesis that there is now only one black spot in the field of vision.

But we need not say, as Cardinal Newman did, that certitude is "indefectible" and permanent—that "whoever loses his conviction on a given point is thereby proved not to have been certain of it." [20] For definition (7), like our other definitions, should be thought of as containing a temporal reference. Even if a man in the position Schlick describes above is *now* certain of the proposition expressed by "There is only one black spot in the field of vision," a proposition about what is to be seen today, he will not be certain about today's black spots tomorrow. And it may well be that at some later date this true proposition about today will become unreasonable.

---

[19] Moritz Schlick, "Facts and Propositions," *Analysis*, II (1935), 70. Compare Norman Malcolm on "the strong sense of 'know,'" in "Knowledge and Belief," *Mind*, LXI (1952), 178–189.

[20] *The Grammar of Assent*, ch. vii.

Epistemic Terms

We need not say that people are certain of all those propositions which they know to be true or which they perceive to be true. A man may know or perceive that there is smoke along the harbor without being certain—for there may be other propositions which, for him, are even more worthy of belief. In one of its many senses, "There *appears* to me to be smoke along the harbor," if it is true, expresses a proposition which, for any subject, no matter what he may be perceiving, is more acceptable than the proposition that there *is* smoke there. This point, which I shall discuss in more detail in subsequent chapters, is sometimes obscured by the other uses which "certain," "know," and "appear" happen to have in ordinary discourse.

It would be strange to say, "Not only do I *know* that that is true—I am *certain* of it." For one way of saying, "I am certain," in the present sense of the word, is to say, "I know," with emphasis.[21] Moreover, the negative expression "I am *not* certain that . . ." is often used to mean, not simply "It is false that I am certain that . . . ," but, more strongly, "I do not believe, and am indeed inclined to doubt, that . . ." I may say, "I'm not certain I can attend the meeting," in order to convey my belief that I probably won't attend the meeting. But in saying above that *knowing* and *perceiving* do not imply *being certain*, I mean merely that there are some propositions which are even more worthy of our belief than many of those which we know or perceive to be true.

---

[21] A. D. Woozely contrasts this "certifying" or "guaranteeing" character of "I know that" with the tentativeness expressed by "I am certain," when "I am certain" means merely that I feel sure; see his *Theory of Knowledge* (London, 1949), pp. 187–189. Compare J. L. Austin, "Other Minds," *Proceedings of the Aristotelian Society*, suppl. vol. XX (1946), especially pp. 170–174, reprinted in Antony Flew, ed., *Logic and Language*, 2d ser. In "Ordinary Language and Absolute Certainty," Paul Edwards points out ambiguities in uses of "certain" (*Philosophical Studies*, I [1950]).

Two

Probability and Evidence

1. The terms "probable" and "likely," in their ordinary use, are closely related to our epistemic terms. Saying that a statement or hypothesis is *probable*—"more probable than not"— may be very much like saying that it is *evident*, in the sense of "evident" defined in the previous chapter. Saying that a statement or hypothesis is *improbable* may be very much like saying that it is *unreasonable*. And saying that one statement or hypothesis is *more probable than* another may be very much like saying that the one is *more worthy of belief* than the other. But probability expressions also have two technical uses, definable in mathematical and logical terms, without reference to any epistemic term or to the ethics of belief. I shall refer to these two uses of probability expression as their *inductive* and their *statistical* uses.[1] In the present chapter, I shall consider,

[1] These two uses are clearly distinguished in Rudolf Carnap, *Logical Foundations of Probability*, and in J. O. Urmson, "Two of the Senses of 'Probable,'" *Analysis*, vol. VIII (1947). Toulmin has pointed out that it would be a mistake to identify either of these technical uses with the ordinary use of "probable"; but we shall see, nevertheless, that there

somewhat briefly, the following question: What is the epistemic significance of these two technical uses of probability expressions?

2. We use probability expressions *inductively* when we talk about the probability that a statement or hypothesis may have *in relation to* other statements or hypotheses. In this use, "probable" and "improbable," like "near" and "far," are relative terms. For a statement *h* may be *probable* in relation to certain statements or premises *e*, but *improbable* in relation to certain *other* statements or premises *e'*. For example, the statement

(*h*) John is a native

is probable in relation to

(*e*) Eighty per cent of the merchants are natives and John is a merchant

and improbable in relation to

(*e'*) Ninety-nine per cent of the natives can speak the language and John cannot.

In recent studies of the logic of inductive probability (sometimes called the logic of *confirmation*), it has been suggested that, merely by ascertaining the logical properties of any statements, *e, h,* and *i,* of certain artificial languages, one can determine whether *h* is probable in relation to *e* and whether *h* is more probable than *i* in relation to *e*.[2] Our three state-

is a sense in which we may interpret the ordinary epistemic use of "probable" in terms of these technical uses. See Stephen Toulmin, "Probability," *Proceedings of the Aristotelian Society*, suppl. vol. XXIV (1950), reprinted in Antony Flew, ed., *Essays in Conceptual Analysis*.

[2] See Carnap, *op. cit.*; C. G. Hempel, "A Purely Syntactical Definition of Confirmation," *Journal of Symbolic Logic*, VIII (1943), 122–143; and C. G. Hempel and Paul Oppenheim, "A Definition of 'Degree of Confirmation,'" *Philosophy of Science*, XII (1945), 98–115.

ments above may illustrate this point. If the three terms, "John," "merchant," and "native," which occur in the three statements, are replaced, completely and consistently and in accordance with the rules of grammar, by any other three terms, then we derive three new statements such that the first is probable in relation to the second and improbable in relation to the third. If this description of inductive probability is accurate, then, for certain artificial languages at least, the term "probable," in its inductive use, could be said to express a purely *logical* concept. And in such a case, a probability statement—a statement saying that, in relation to some premise *e*, some hypothesis *h* is probable, or improbable, or more probable than some other hypothesis—is a purely logical statement, and hence a statement the truth of which can be determined by reference solely to logical considerations. But whether or not this conception of inductive probability is accurate, inductive probability statements perform their practical function, as a "guide of life," only when they satisfy two *epistemic* conditions.

3.   When we *apply* the logic of inductive probability, we appeal to a probability relation to show that some hypothesis or statement is evident (and hence that its contradictory is unreasonable) or to show that some statement or hypothesis is acceptable and hence not unreasonable. Let us suppose, for example, that we are interested in the hypothesis *h*—"John is a native"—cited above and wish to decide whether it is evident. We know that *h* is probable in relation to the premise *e*—"Eighty per cent of the merchants are natives and John is a merchant." But this information, which concerns only relations between statements or propositions, does not enable us to decide whether we have adequate evidence for *h*. If *e* happened to be a statement which is *unreasonable*, we would not

appeal to *e* in order to show that *h* is evident. And if *e* were merely acceptable but not evident, appeal to *e* would not be sufficient to show that *h* is evident; for in such a case, our premise *e* would be *indifferent* and therefore its contradictory would also be acceptable.

It is sometimes said that, when we use inductive probability to decide whether or not some particular hypothesis is evident, we should appeal only to premises of which we are *certain*. But this requirement seems more strict than necessary. I suggest that the application of probability requires only that our premises be statements for which we have *adequate evidence*.[3]

In writings on the logic of inductive probability, this first epistemic condition is usually acknowledged by assuming that the subject who is applying the logic has available to him premises which express his "knowledge of the results of his observations." [4] Sometimes the word "knowledge" is avoided in such writings; the word "observe" may be then interpreted epistemically, as synonymous with the epistemic sense of "perceive," as defined in the previous chapter.

4. A second epistemic condition for the application of probability is suggested by Jacob Bernoulli's maxim that, when calculating a probability, we should take account of all the evidence that is available to us.[5] Suppose, for example, we wish to make a decision concerning the hypothesis *h*, "John is a native," and that we have adequate evidence, not only for the proposition *e*, "Eighty per cent of the merchants are natives and John is one of the merchants," but *also for* the proposition

---

[3] Compare Nelson Goodman, "Sense and Certainty," *Philosophical Review*, LXI (1952), especially 162–163.

[4] See Donald Williams, *The Ground of Induction* (Cambridge, 1947), pp. 167–168, and Carnap, *op. cit., passim.*

[5] See J. M. Keynes, A *Treatise on Probability*, pp. 76, 322.

e', "Ninety-nine per cent of the natives can speak the language and John cannot." If we were to base our decision solely upon *e*, we would not be making proper application of the theory of probability, despite the fact that we have adequate evidence for *e* and that *h* is probable in relation to *e*. For clearly the premises we use in this application of probability should include *e'*—a statement for which we also have adequate evidence and whose probability relation to our hypothesis *h* is quite different from that of *e* to *h*.

In the *Logical Foundations of Probability*, Carnap formulates the "requirement of total evidence" in this way: "In the application of inductive logic to a given knowledge situation, the total evidence available must be taken as basis for determining the degree of confirmation." [6] But it is hardly possible for anyone to consider, every time he applies the theory of probability, *all* of the propositions for which he has adequate evidence. I suggest, therefore, that a less rigid requirement would be better. We could say, for example, that whenever anyone applies inductive probability he should not omit any premises which he believes would affect the probability of the conclusion. More exactly: suppose a man is applying inductive probability in order to make a decision concerning some hypothesis *h* and that the premises he has so far considered are *e*; if he has adequate evidence for another statement *e'* and if he believes that the probability which *h* bears to the conjunction of *e* and *e'* is different from that which *h* bears to *e*, then he should include *e'* among his premises.

---

[6] Carnap, *op. cit.*, p. 211. In *The Ground and Nature of the Right*, C. I. Lewis formulates the requirement in this way: "No inductive conclusion is well taken and justly credible unless the obligation to muster the given and available evidence has been met" (p. 32). In *Human Knowledge*, Bertrand Russell suggests that our premises should embrace "all the *known* relevant evidence" (p. 498; my italics).

Probability and Evidence

The expression "in all probability" is often used to indicate that this second epistemic requirement has been met.

Before we *act upon* any hypothesis meeting these two epistemic conditions we should also consider whether *additional* inquiry or investigation is indicated (see Chapter One, Section 4). If we plan a minor operation, one specialist may be enough; but if we plan a major operation, we should call in others. It would be difficult, I believe, to formulate a rule telling us the conditions under which such inquiry or investigation *is* indicated. But if we are ever justified in acting at all, then there are times when we are justified in acting upon the evidence that happens to be on hand.

5. In their *statistical* use, probability terms may convey nothing of epistemic significance. If we say, "The probability is .69 that a forty-year-old resident of Scotland can swim," using "probability" in its statistical sense, our statement has no implications about what anyone knows or has adequate evidence for believing. For it is merely a translation of some statistical statement—some such statement as "Sixty-nine per cent of the forty-year-old residents of Scotland can swim." If we wish to make a decision concerning the ability of some particular resident of Scotland, we should not appeal to the statistical statement—or to its translation in terms of probability—unless the statistical statement is evident or at least acceptable. And even if we have adequate evidence for the statistical statement, it will not perform its proper function unless we consider it in the way described above, with the other relevant evidence we believe to be at hand. In short, a statement using "probability" in its statistical sense should function as a "guide of life" only when it is a premise in an *inductive* probability relation which meets the two epistemic conditions we have just described.

27

6. We may say, then, that although probability terms, in their two technical uses, need not be defined epistemically, they do function epistemically when they are properly *applied* in any practical situation. The result of such application is that the expressions "probable," "improbable," and "more probable than" will function very much like our three epistemic expressions "evident," "unreasonable," and "more worthy of belief than." If a statement is probable in relation to the total evidence of any subject S, then the statement is at least acceptable for S.[7] If a statement is improbable in relation to the total evidence of any subject S, then it is one which is unreasonable for S. And if one statement is more probable than another in relation to the total evidence of any subject S, then the one is more worthy of S's belief than is the other.[8]

If it were possible to assign *degrees* to the probability which a given hypothesis has in relation to a man's total evidence, then we should say that the hypothesis is epistemically *indifferent* for him only if it has a probability of .50 in relation to that evidence. And we should say that the hypothesis is evident if it has a probability greater than .50 and unreasonable if it has a probability less than .50. But, although it is possible to

---

[7] We may say, for the present, that the locution "*h* is probable in relation to the *total evidence* of S" means that *h* is probable in relation to the conjunction of all those statements for which S has adequate evidence. In Chapter Six I shall suggest a somewhat more satisfactory way of defining this locution.

[8] Writers on inductive probability are not in agreement concerning what should be the proper method of choosing among the possible logical definitions of "probable," or "degree of confirmation"; a clear statement of this problem may be found in John W. Lenz, "Carnap on Defining 'Degree of Confirmation,'" *Philosophy of Science*, XXIII (1956), 230–236. I suggest that no such definition is adequate unless it provides a sense of "probable" such that the final three statements of the above paragraph, when interpreted in that sense, remain true. In the chapters that follow, I discuss some of the problems which would be involved in deciding whether any definition does meet this epistemic condition.

assign degrees to the probability which some hypotheses have in relation to certain types of premise, it is in fact unlikely that degrees can be assigned in any acceptable way to the probability which any hypothesis has in relation to the *total evidence* of any particular subject.[9]

The mathematical theory of probability and the logic of confirmation, or inductive probability, tell us how to *extend* our application of "evidence." That is to say, they tell us the conditions under which, given an application of "evidence" to a set of premises, we can apply it to still other hypotheses— hypotheses which are probable in relation to those premises. The theory of probability may be compared with a financial sheet that tells us how to increase our savings. The financial sheet is of no practical use unless we have some savings to invest. And we cannot apply the theory of probability until we are able to apply the term "evidence."

In what follows, then, I shall discuss the application of "evidence" without further reference to probability or confirmation.

---

[9] The problem of assigning degrees to inductive probability is discussed in detail in Carnap, *op. cit.*, ch. iv, sec. 48, and ch. v. In *Human Knowledge*, Russell discusses the problem of determining the probability of a given hypothesis in relation to a subject's total evidence. If I wish to determine the probability of a hypothesis about how long I will live, Russell notes, it will not be enough for me to consider what I know of statistical tables. "Every circumstance of my health and my way of life is relevant, but some of these may be so uncommon that I can get no reliable help from statistics. . . . The probability at which I finally arrive is thus something quite vague and quite incapable of numerical measurement; but it is upon this vague probability that, as a disciple of Bishop Butler, I have to act" (p. 342).

Three

The Problem of "the Criterion"

1. The philosophy of perception, to which we shall turn in Part II of this book, is concerned in part with the *application* of epistemic terms. How are we to identify an instance of "adequate evidence"? To what situations may we apply our locution "S has adequate evidence for *h*"? The problem to which these questions give rise is best introduced, I think, by considering briefly its analogue in moral philosophy.

How do we identify an instance of "rightness"? If we say, of some particular act, that that act is *right* and if we are prepared to defend our statement, then we are prepared to appeal to some characteristic *in virtue of which* the act is right. Possibly we are prepared to show that the act is an instance of courage, or of forgiveness, or that it is motivated by a wish to decrease the amount of pain in the world. If we succeed in showing that the act is right, then the characteristic to which we appeal, whatever it may be, is one such that *every* act to which it applies is an act which is right, or which "tends to be right." But the characteristic is not one we need to describe or identify in distinctly *ethical* terms. If we wish to point out that someone is motivated by the wish to decrease the amount of pain in the world, or that he is acting courageously, we can convey what we want to convey without using "right" or "good" or "ought" or any other ethical term. Let us say that the characteristic to which we appeal is one which is "right-making." [1]

There are three important points to be made about "right-making" characteristics. (1) A "right-making" characteristic is one that can be described and identified in ethically neutral language—without the use of ethical terms. (2) When we find out, or when we show, that a particular act is right, we find out, or show, that it has some "right-making" characteristic. And (3) every act that is right is right *in virtue of* some "right-making" characteristic which the act has—some characteristic such that every act which has that characteristic is right, or "tends to be right." Similar points may be made, *mutatis mutandis*, of such ethical terms as "wrong," "good," and "bad."

Among the traditional tasks of moral philosophy is that of describing characteristics which are "right-making," "wrong-making," "good-making," and the like. In listing such characteristics, the moral philosopher is not providing *definitions* of the ethical terms concerned. We may say, following one ancient usage, that he is providing *criteria* for applying these terms.

---

[1] "Moral characteristics are always dependent upon certain other characteristics which can be described in purely neutral non-moral terms. Let us call those non-moral characteristics whose presence in anything confers rightness or goodness on it *right-making* and *wrong-making* characteristics. And let us define *good-making* and *bad-making* characteristics in a similar way" (C. D. Broad, "Some of the Main Problems of Ethics," *Philosophy*, XXI [1946], 103). Compare Austin Duncan-Jones, *Butler's Moral Philosophy* (Harmondsworth, 1952), ch. viii, secs. 1 and 2, and R. M. Hare, *The Language of Morals* (Oxford, 1952), pp. 80 ff.

Perceiving

Our problem—"the problem of the criterion"—is that of finding similar criteria for applying "adequate evidence." If we find such criteria, any "evidence-bearing" characteristics, we must not suppose that a description of them would constitute a *definition* of "evidence." [2]

If a moral philosopher were to say, "I'm trying to find out what characteristics are 'right-making' so that I'll have some way of deciding which actions are right and which are not," he would be, I think, confused. For we shall see that the moral philosopher has no way of deciding which characteristics are "right-making" until he can say which actions are right. The only way of telling whether a characteristic is "right-making" is to determine whether every action to which it applies is an action which is right.[3] And similarly we have no way of deciding which characteristics are "evidence-bearing" until we know which of our beliefs are evident.

Descartes, it is true, professed to be looking for a way of telling which of his beliefs are evident and which not—a method by means of which he could distinguish knowledge from mere opinion. But his description of his quest does not tell us how he *found* such a method; it implies, rather, that he was already able to make such distinctions when he began. In his reply to

---

[2] In the *Problem of Knowledge* (London, 1956), A. J. Ayer defines "knowledge" in terms of "the right to be sure" and then notes that it would be a mistake to transform a description of the ways of earning this right into a definition of knowing (p. 34). In this passage Ayer is conscious of the problem of the criterion; but it is fair to say, I think, that he does not provide us with any solution. Sextus Empiricus discussed the problem of "the criterion" in bks. I and II of his *Outlines of Pyrrhonism*.

[3] According to H. A. Prichard this mistake is typical of moral philosophy and a similar mistake is typical of the theory of knowledge. See his "Does Moral Philosophy Rest on a Mistake?" *Mind*, vol. XXI (1912), reprinted in *Moral Obligation* and in W. S. Sellars and John Hospers, *Readings in Ethical Theory* (New York, 1952).

the Seventh Set of Objections, he proposes a "homely example" about a man and a basket of apples. If a man

> had a basket of apples and, fearing that some of them were rotten, wanted to take those out lest they might make the rest go wrong, how could he do that? Would he not first turn the whole of the apples out of the basket and look them over one by one, and then having selected those which he saw not to be rotten, place them again in the basket and leave out the others? [4]

In the *Discourse on Method*, Descartes had said, in effect, that he wanted to *find* a way of identifying good and bad apples *in order that* he might be able to decide which ones *are* good and which bad. But in the present passage, he assumes that he already has a way of telling which apples are good and which bad, he has only to look them over and see.

"The problem of the criterion" is that of describing certain of the conditions under which we may *apply* our epistemic vocabulary—and, more particularly, that of describing certain of the conditions under which we may apply our locution "S has adequate evidence for *h*." In setting this problem for ourselves, we do not presuppose, nor should we presuppose, that there are certain conditions—certain "evidence-bearing" characteristics—which people *look for* in order to decide whether they have evidence for their beliefs. The grammarian, similarly, may try to describe the conditions under which, say, people use the imperfect tense rather than the past perfect; but in so doing, he does not mean to imply that, before using this tense, people think

---

[4] E. S. Haldane and R. T. Ross, eds., *The Philosophical Works of Descartes* (Cambridge, 1934), II, 282. In pt. II of the *Discourse on Method*, Descartes uses a slightly different figure: "My design was only to provide myself with good ground for assurance, and to reject the quicksand and mud in order to find the rock or clay" (Haldane and Ross, eds., I, 99).

about these conditions or try to decide whether or not they apply.

2. Hobbes said, "The inn of evidence has no sign-board." But I suggest that, whenever a man has adequate evidence for some proposition or hypothesis, he is in a state which constitutes a *mark of evidence* for that proposition or hypothesis.

What, then, would be a "mark of evidence" for a proposition or hypothesis *h?* In asking this question, we are asking: What would be a *criterion* by means of which a particular subject S might apply our locution "S has adequate evidence for *h*"? As there were three points to be made about "right-making" characteristics, there are three points to be made about marks of evidence—about "evidence-bearing" characteristics.

(1) A mark or criterion, for any subject S, that S has adequate evidence for a given proposition or hypothesis *h*, would be some state or condition of S which could be described without using "know," or "perceive," or "evident," or any other epistemic term. It would be a condition we could describe in "epistemically neutral" sentences—sentences which do not logically entail any sentence saying of anyone that he has (or that he doesn't have) adequate evidence for any proposition.[5]

(2) Should we say that a mark for S, that S has adequate evidence for a given proposition or hypothesis *h*, would be some state or condition to which S appeals when he wishes to *show* that he has evidence for *h*—or some state or condition which he *discovers* to hold when he discovers he has adequate evidence for *h*? The words "discover" and "show," in this present use, are themselves epistemic terms. To *discover* that some condition holds is, among other things, to acquire adequate evidence for believing that it does; and to *show* some other person that some

---

[5] This way of characterizing "epistemically neutral" language was suggested to me by Professor Richard Brandt.

condition holds is, among other things, to enable him to have adequate evidence for believing that it does. If we are to formulate our second requirement in "epistemically neutral" language, I believe we must say something like this: A mark or criterion, for any subject S, that S has adequate evidence for a given proposition or hypothesis *h*, would be some state or condition of S which is such that S could not make any mistake at any time about his *being* in that state or condition at that time; that is to say, S could not believe falsely at any time either that he is in that state at that time or that he is not in that state at that time.[6] Certain types of *believing* would satisfy this second requirement. A man cannot be mistaken, for example, with respect to what is asserted by his sentence, "I believe the library is west of the bell tower." But we shall appeal to somewhat different marks of evidence.

(3) Finally, a mark or criterion, for any subject S, that S has adequate evidence for a given proposition or hypothesis *h*, would be a state or condition such that, whenever S is in that state or condition, S has adequate evidence for *h*. In virtue of (1), we can describe such a mark in sentences which do not *logically entail* that S has adequate evidence for *h*; but, in virtue of (3), these sentences will *imply* that he does.

Philosophers have proposed various criteria, or marks, of evidence, but in many cases their proposals fail to meet one or more of our three conditions.

We cannot be content to say, as apparently some philosophers would be, that a man has adequate evidence for any proposition he *knows*, or *remembers*, or *sees*, or *perceives* to be true. If a man *sees* that there is a cat on the roof, then, clearly, he has

---

[6] In "Propositions, Truth, and the Ultimate Criterion of Truth," C. J. Ducasse describes the "ultimate undisbelievability" of certain propositions as being a mark of their evidence (*Philosophy and Phenomenological Research*, IV (1944), especially 337–340).

adequate evidence for the proposition that there is a cat on the roof. This type of criterion does not meet the first of our three conditions, however. For "see," "know," "remember," and "perceive," as here used, are epistemic terms—terms which are definable by means of our locution "S ought to place more confidence in h than in i."

It has been suggested that we have adequate evidence for any proposition which is accepted by "the scientists of our culture circle." [7] It has also been suggested that we have adequate evidence for any proposition "revealed to us by God." Possibly the words "scientist" and "revealed," in these criteria, fail to conform to our first condition. In any case, both criteria fail to meet the second condition. We are all quite capable of believing falsely at any time that a given proposition is accepted by the scientists of our culture circle at that time or has been revealed to us by God at that time.

According to Descartes, we have adequate evidence for those propositions "we conceive very clearly and very distinctly." This criterion does not seem to meet our third condition. For we can conceive very clearly and very distinctly what is expressed by many statements we know to be false.

In *The Logic of Chance*, Venn seems to suggest that *surprise* is a mark of evidence.[8] Surprise is a state we can describe without using any epistemic terms; I think we may say that no one can believe falsely at any time either that he is surprised at that

---

[7] Some of the early writings of the members of the Vienna Circle may be interpreted as proposing such a criterion. See Otto Neurath, "Radikaler Physikalismus und 'Wirkliche Welt,'" *Erkenntnis*, IV (1934), 346–362, and C. G. Hempel, "On the Logical Positivists' Theory of Truth," *Analysis*, II (1935), 49–59.

[8] "Hence our surprise, though, as stated above, having no proper claim to admission into the science of Probability, is such a constant and regular accompaniment of that which probability is concerned with, that notice must often be taken of it" (John Venn, *The Logic of Chance* [London and Cambridge, 1866], ch. iii, sec. 30; compare sec. 29).

time or that he is not surprised at that time; and perhaps we may say that, if a man is surprised, he has adequate evidence for the hypothesis that one of his beliefs is mistaken. A traveler believing himself to be in the South Pacific may be surprised in seeing—or in thinking that he is seeing—an iceberg. Hence he has adequate evidence for the hypothesis that one of his beliefs is mistaken: his belief that he is in the South Pacific, his belief that there are no icebergs in the South Pacific, or his belief that he is seeing an iceberg. But the state of surprise does not indicate *which one* of his beliefs should be rejected.

Are there any states that provide us with more satisfactory marks of evidence? In the chapters that follow I will attempt to describe a number of such states.

3.   We have seen that in moral philosophy it is useful to distinguish between an *absolute* and a *practical* sense of "right" and of "ought." We can never know, with respect to any particular act, whether it is right in the absolute sense of "right"; for we can never know what the totality of its effects will turn out to be. But we can know whether the act is praiseworthy; we can know whether it is right in the practical sense of "right." We may hope that there is some natural connection between what is practically and absolutely right—that most of those acts that are practically right are also absolutely right, or, in Kant's terms, that observance of the moral law will promote the *summum bonum*.[9] I have said that the "ought" in terms of which we have discussed the ethics of belief is the practical "ought"

---

[9] See bk. II, ch. ii, of *The Critique of Practical Reason*, on "the antinomy of practical reason" and its solution. It is to insure "a natural and necessary connexion between the consciousness of morality and the expectation of a proportionate happiness as its result"—a natural and necessary connection between practical rightness and absolute rightness—that practical reason, according to Kant, postulates the existence of God and the immortality of the soul.

and not the absolute "ought." Here, too, we may hope that there is a connection between what is practically right and what is absolutely right.

We hope, in other words, that our marks of *evidence* will also be marks of *truth*. We hope that, if there is some general mark of evidence, a certain type of state M which is a mark of evidence for a certain type of hypothesis H, then M will be a reliable criterion of truth; we hope that, more often than not, when we believe H while we are in state M, we will believe H truly.

I have noted that an inductive argument—an application of probability theory—does not provide us with evidence for any hypothesis unless we make use of premises for which we have adequate evidence. Once we have such premises, however, we may *then* inductively confirm (or disconfirm) the hypothesis that a certain mark of evidence is also a mark of truth; we may inductively confirm (or disconfirm) the hypothesis that, more often than not, when S believes an H hypothesis while he is in state M, he believes the H hypothesis truly. To a certain extent, therefore, our hope that we can find a "natural connexion" between our marks of evidence and marks of truth may be capable of fulfillment. We cannot "test" every mark of evidence in this way unless we reason in a circle. But even if we do thus reason in a circle, we may take some comfort if by so doing we find that induction does not discredit the marks of evidence of its premises.[10]

---

[10] Compare C. S. Peirce, *Collected Papers*, 5.384, 5.591–592. When Cardinal Mercier discussed "marks of truth" in his *Critériologie générale*, he had in mind, I believe, what I have called "marks of evidence which are also marks of truth." He formulated three requirements—those of being "internal," "immediate," and "objective"—which any such mark or criterion must meet. In saying that the criterion must be "internal," that it is something the subject can find in himself (*"en lui-même"*), he was saying, what I have said above, that a mark of evidence is a state

The Problem of "the Criterion"

If the word "hope," as it is used above, does not seem strong enough, one might use "animal faith." Or one might use Kantian terms and say: in knowing and in perceiving, we "postulate" that certain marks of evidence are also marks of truth. The status of this postulate—or hope—will become clearer, I believe, in the chapters that follow.

---

of the subject; in saying that the criterion must be "immediate," he had in mind, I believe, what I have formulated as the second condition above; and in saying that it must be "objective," he was saying, I believe, that it should be a mark of truth as well as a mark of evidence. Although Mercier was sensitive to the charge of circularity, I doubt that the criterion he finally proposed (our judgments are true provided that their subjects and predicates *manifest* or *express* reality) satisfies my first condition above; for "express" and "manifest," as he interpreted them, seem to be epistemic terms, whose meanings can be conveyed only through the use of such terms as "know," "evident," or "perceive." See D. J. Mercier, *Critériologie générale*, 8th ed. (Louvain, 1923), pp. 234, 415–423.

PART II

Evidence

Four

Three Uses of Appear Words

1.   By considering the word "appears" as it is intended in the first of our definitions—the definition of the propositional sense of "perceive"—we will be led to one mark of evidence. According to that definition a man *perceives* something to have a certain characteristic, or perceives *that* the thing has the characteristic, provided, first, he takes the thing to have the characteristic, secondly, he has adequate evidence for so doing, and, thirdly, the thing *appears* to him in some way.

Appear words—"appear," "seem," "look," "sound," "feel," "smell," and the like—have many uses, and we shall find in subsequent chapters that some of these uses involve us in additional philosophical questions. In the present chapter we will restrict ourselves to those features of their ordinary use which happen to throw light upon the problem of "the criterion."

2.   If I say that the ship "appears to be moving," or that it "looks as though" or "sounds as though" it were moving, using the appear words in one familiar way, then it may be inferred

that I believe, or that I am inclined to believe, that the ship *is* moving. When appear words are used in this way, then such locutions as "*x* appears to S to be so-and-so" and "*x* appears so-and-so to S" may be taken to imply that the subject S believes, or is inclined to believe, that *x is* so-and-so. And I think that, in this same use, they may be also taken to imply that the subject S has *adequate evidence* for believing that *x* is so-and-so. What is expressed by "The ship seems to me to be moving" may also be expressed by "*Apparently*—or *evidently*—the ship is moving." Let us refer to this use of appear words as their *epistemic* use.[1]

The locutions "*x* appears to S to be so-and-so" and "*x* appears so-and-so to S" sometimes do *not* imply that the subject S believes, or is even inclined to believe, that *x* is so-and-so. I tell the oculist that the letters on his chart "now appear to run together" because both of us know that they do not run together. And when people point out that straight sticks sometimes "look bent" in water, that loud things "sound faint" from far away, that parallel tracks often "appear to converge," or "look convergent," that square things "look diamond-shaped" when approached obliquely, they do not believe that these things have the characteristics which they appear to have. In these instances "*x* appears so-and-so" does not mean that *x* is apparently so-and-so.

It must not be supposed, however, that appear words, in this second use, imply the negations of the corresponding sentences about believing. I may tell the oculist, when he has changed the lenses, that the letters "no longer appear to run together." And one may say that the stick "looks straight again now that it is

---

[1] In a review of A. J. Ayer's *The Foundations of Empirical Knowledge* (*Mind*, L [1941], 293), H. H. Price refers to the "epistemic use" of appear words and distinguishes this use from other uses. Compare C. D. Broad, *Scientific Thought* (London, 1923), pp. 236–237, and A. M. Quinton, "The Problem of Perception," *Mind*, LXIV (1955), 28–51.

out of the water," that from some points of view square things "look square," that loud whistles often "sound loud," and that many parallel lines "do not appear to converge."

Using appear words in the present nonepistemic sense, we may say that the railroad tracks "look convergent" if they look the way two converging lines would ordinarily be expected to look if both were visible at once. A photograph faithfully representing the way the railroad tracks look would contain two lines that *are* convergent. If we can say that the rectangular table-top "looks diamond-shaped" from one corner of the room, then a photograph taken from that corner of the room will contain a figure that is diamond-shaped. For the point of the locution "*x* appears so-and-so," in its present sense, is to compare *x* with things that *are* so-and-so. Let us speak, then, of the *comparative* use of appear words.

When we use appear words comparatively, the locution

x appears to S to be . . .

and its variants may be interpreted as comparing *x* with those things which have the characteristic that *x* is said to appear to have. A more explicit rendering of such locutions, therefore, would be something like this:

x appears to S in the way in which things that are . . . appear under conditions which are. . . .

The way in which we should complete the reference to conditions in the second part this locution varies, depending upon the conditions under which the appear sentence is made. In some cases, "That thing appears red," when intended in its comparative sense, may mean the same as "That thing appears in the way in which red things might normally be expected to appear." In other cases, it may mean, more explicitly, that the thing appears in the way in which red things might normally be expected to appear *under present* conditions; in still other cases, it may mean that the thing appears in the way in which red things might normally be expected to appear under *ordinary*, or *more usual*, conditions. And occasionally "That thing appears red" may mean that the thing appears in the way in which red things would appear under "optimum conditions"—under the conditions which are "most favorable" for perceiving such things.[2] In most cases, the context in which a comparative appear sentence is uttered will enable us to determine what types of conditions are intended.[3] But, however these conditions are to be described, the essential point about the comparative use of "appears so-and-so" is that the sentences in which it is to be found can be translated into other sentences referring to things which *are* so-and-so.

Using "appear" in its comparative sense, we may say that the

---

[2] What these "optimum" or "most favorable" conditions are varies considerably, depending upon the type of predicate which we say that x appears to have. Some of these conditions are indicated in the following quotation: "A thing is said to 'look round' when it presents the quale [appearance] which a really round object does when held at right angles to the line of vision; and a thing is said to 'look blue' when it looks the way a really blue thing does under usual or standard illumination. In general, the name of the property is also assigned to the appearance of it under certain optimum conditions. The penny *looks* round when held at that angle at which judgment of actual shape from visual appearance is safest. And an object *looks* the color that it is under that illumination which is conducive to accurate discrimination. A thing looks as big as it is at about that distance (for objects of its size) at which human beings make fewest mistakes in judgments of magnitude" (C. I. Lewis, *Mind and the World-Order* [New York, 1929], pp. 122–123). I think that this passage is mistaken only in its suggestion that "x appears . . . ," in its comparative use, may *always* be translated as "x appears the way in which things that are . . . appear under optimum conditions for viewing things which are. . . ."

[3] But when philosophers make statements about "things appearing the way they really are," using appear in its comparative sense, they would be well advised, I think, to translate their statements into explicit comparative statements having the form illustrated above.

way things appear to us depends, not only on the nature of the things, but also on the conditions under which we perceive them. The things we perceive may be made to appear in different ways merely by varying the conditions of observation or by distorting our perceptual apparatus.

The same water which feels very hot when poured on inflamed spots seems lukewarm to us. And the same honey seems chilly to the old but mild to those in their prime, and similarly the same sound seems to the former faint, but to the latter clearly audible. The same wine which seems sour to those who have previously eaten dates or figs seems sweet to those who have just consumed nuts or chick-peas; and the vestibule of the bath-house which warms those entering from the outside chills those coming out.[4]

These ancient examples remind us that there is a close connection between the "epistemic" and "comparative" uses of appear words; for the sentences in which the examples are described may be taken in either or in both of these senses. In saying that water "feels hot" to the man whose skin is inflamed, our philosopher may be telling us both (a) that the water feels the way hot water might normally be expected to feel and (b) that the man who feels it takes it to *be* hot—that he believes, say, that the water is ready to boil. We often use appear locutions in their epistemic sense because of the fact that we can also apply them in their comparative sense. A man who is not a professional winetaster may find that his wine looks and tastes like Burgundy and conclude, on the basis of this finding, "Apparently it is Burgundy." But we may also use "appear" in its epistemic sense when we would not use it in its comparative sense. One may say, on a hilltop, "The roads appear to be parallel" because the roads, like railroad tracks, appear to converge.

---

[4] Sextus Empiricus, *Outlines of Pyrrhonism*, bk. I, abridged from pp. 55, 65, and 63 of vol. I of *Sextus Empiricus* (Loeb Classical Library).

Ordinarily the context in which an appear statement is made will tell us whether the appear words are to be taken epistemically or comparatively. But the statements made by philosophers and psychologists are sometimes unclear in this respect. The following statement, describing the familiar phenomenon of perceptual constancy, is true if "appear" is taken in its epistemic sense but false if it is taken in its comparative sense.

As I stand to one side and look at the top of a circular table, it does not appear as the narrow ellipse that its retinal image is, that the artist would sketch in his projection of the scene. Although every room is full of rectangles, they are perceived not as various diamonds and distorted rectangles, but approximately in their true proportions. The brain corrects the perception for the angle of projection.[5]

(The expression "are perceived . . . as," which occurs in the second sentence of this quotation, should be read as a synonym for the epistemic sense of "appear to be," but not as a synonym for "are perceived to be" or for the comparative sense of "appear to be.")

3.   I have tried to describe our comparative use of "appears so-and-so" by our use of "is so-and-so." Any sentence with an appear word—"appear," "seem," "look," "sound," "feel," "smell," "taste"—used in its comparative sense may be translated into a sentence describing the way in which a certain type of physical thing appears. More specifically, any sentence containing an expression that describes the way in which something appears, in the comparative sense of "appear," must be capable of translation into another sentence with that expression used

---

[5] E. G. Boring, "The Perception of Objects," *American Journal of Physics*, XIV (1946), 99. Compare Gilbert Ryle's statement: "Round plates, however steeply tilted, do not usually look elliptical" (*The Concept of Mind* [London], 1949, p. 216). We must also beware of the philosophical question, "Does the thing appear the way it really is?"

Three Uses of Appear Words

to describe a property or characteristic of some physical thing. "That apple looks red from here," when intended in this way, may be taken as short for "The apple looks the way you would expect a red apple to look." In the first sentence, "red" seems to designate a way of appearing; in the second, it designates a property or characteristic of certain apples.[6] To know that an apple looks red, in the comparative sense of "look," one must know something about red things—something about the way in which red things would ordinarily look. If there were a man who knew nothing of red things, he could never tell, merely by looking, that anything looks red. If you knew nothing of Arabian music, you could never tell, merely by listening to someone play, whether or not his music happens to "sound Arabian."

The foregoing might be summarized in the following way: The locution "appears so-and-so," in its ordinary comparative sense, may be defined as meaning the same as some locution describing the way in which things that *are* so-and-so appear. Hence we cannot know how to apply "appears so-and-so," in this sense, until we know how to apply "so-and-so." And therefore, if we are not familiar with things that are so-and-so, we may be quite uncertain, on any given occasion, whether anything is appearing so-and-so.

These conclusions are of philosophical interest because each one seems to be inconsistent with what philosophers in the empirical tradition have said about appearing. Indeed, we might describe *empiricism*, in one of the many senses of this word, in terms of beliefs which would seem to contradict what we have just said. We could say—with some oversimplification—that, according to the *empirical* view of the genesis of our knowledge, the following propositions are true:

"(a) If there is a predicate 'so-and-so,' which is commonly

---

[6] I shall discuss certain features of the "grammar" of these uses of adjectives in Chapters Eight and Nine.

49

applied, both to ways of appearing and to the properties of things, as 'red' is applied both to apples and to the way such apples generally look, then the property use of 'so-and-so' may be defined in terms of '*appears* so-and-so.' The predicate 'red,' for example, as it is intended in its ordinary application to such things as apples and roses, may be defined in terms of 'appears red'; an apple may be said to *be* red if and only if it *appears* red under optimum conditions. Hence (b) we cannot know how to apply any such predicate 'so-and-so' until we know how to apply 'appears so-and-so.' We cannot know that an apple is red unless we know either that it sometimes appears red or that something else, which we know to be very much like the apple, sometimes appears red. But (c) even if we should not happen to know whether anything *is* so-and-so, we can be certain, with respect to anything appearing to us, either that it is or that it isn't *appearing* so-and-so. If I do not know whether the apple I'm looking at is red and even if, for some strange reason, I don't happen to know whether anything is red, I can be quite certain either that something now *looks* red to me or that nothing does." [7]

This "empirical" doctrine can be understood only by referring to a third use—the *noncomparative* use—of appear words.

4. When "looks red" is taken in its comparative sense, the statement

(1) The mountainside looks red

entails some statement, of the following sort, about things that *are* red:

(2) The mountainside looks the way red things look in daylight.

---

[7] The first of these theses is discussed in the Appendix, the second in Chapter Nine. Section 4, and the third in Chapter Five, Section 4.

Possibly "in daylight" should be replaced by a different expression; what this expression is may vary from one person to another—depending upon his "language system." The essential point is this: When "looks red" is used comparatively, it may be replaced by an expression of the form "looks the way red things look under . . . conditions," and the statement resulting from such replacement is entailed by the original statement.

But when "looks red" is used *noncomparatively*, in a statement of the form "x looks red," the statement does not *entail* any statement of the form "x looks the way red things look under . . . conditions." If "looks red" is taken noncomparatively in (1), then (1) does not *entail* (2)—even though (1) may be true only if (2) is true.

When "looks red" is used comparatively, the statement

(3) Things which are red look red in daylight

is analytic, for it says, of the way red things look in daylight, only that it is the way red things look in daylight. (The reservation, made above concerning the occurrence of "in daylight" in (2), applies also, of course, to (3).) But when "looks red" is taken *noncomparatively*, (3) is synthetic—an "empirical generalization." [8]

Many other expressions, of the form "appears so-and-so," have comparative and noncomparative uses which may be distinguished in a similar way. Possibly there is no good reason for supposing that, in ordinary language, there is, for each such expression, just one comparative and one noncomparative use, invariant for all people. But I suggest that, for each of us who uses such expressions, there are, for many of these expressions, both

---

[8] The predicate "red," as it is used in (2) and (3), should be taken in its "physical" sense, as referring to the capacity of things to reflect lightwaves of a certain sort. I shall discuss this sense of "red" in Chapter Nine.

comparative and noncomparative uses. The "empirical" view, just described, was formulated in statements using such expressions noncomparatively.

These relations between the comparative and the noncomparative uses of appear words may be further illustrated by contrasting two possible uses of the expression "speaks French." If we define "Frenchman" geographically, as a person who was born in France, we might define "the French language" as the language which is spoken by the majority of Frenchmen; or we might define it by reference to its vocabulary and rules of grammar. In the first case, we would say that the statement

(1′) John speaks French

entails the statement

(2′) John speaks the language spoken by most Frenchmen.

And the statement

(3′) Most Frenchmen speak French

would be analytic. But in the second case, where we define the French language, not by reference to those who speak it, but by reference to its vocabulary and grammar, (1′) does not entail (2′)—even though, in fact, (1′) is true only if (2′) is true. And in this second case, (3′) is synthetic, an "empirical generalization." Anyone who could be said, in the one use, to speak French could also be said, in the other use, to speak French. But a man who knew nothing about the vocabulary and grammar of the language spoken by most Frenchmen might know that one of the two statements, (1′) and (2′), is true, without knowing that the other is also true.

In Chapter Eight, the noncomparative use of appear words will be discussed in more detail. At present we are concerned only with its epistemic significance.

When "The mountainside looks red to me" is taken noncomparatively, it becomes a statement I can know to be true even if I don't happen to know anything about the way in which red things ordinarily appear; I may know that (1) is true without realizing that (2) is also true. More generally, when we take the locution "x appears so-and-so to S" noncomparatively, we can say that the subject S, referred to in such a statement, can know whether the statement is true even if he knows nothing about things which *are* so-and-so.[9] Such statements, as we shall now see, describe marks of evidence.

---

[9] In *An Analysis of Knowledge and Valuation* (LaSalle, Ill., 1946), C. I. Lewis speaks of the "expressive use" of language. Although his terminology is quite different from that used here, I believe that what he means by "expressive use" is the same as what I mean by noncomparative use." But I have tried to discuss these questions without introducing such terms as "the given," "immediate awareness," "direct experience," or "acquaintance." Compare also William Kneale, "Sensation and the Physical World," *Philosophical Quarterly*, I (1951), 151.

Five

Justification and Perception

1. When we wish to *test* or *confirm* a statement, we seek out *new* evidence. We may take a closer look, interview witnesses, and perform experiments. But when we wish to *defend* or *justify* a statement, we appeal to the evidence which happens to be at hand. We weigh the evidence and try to show, in effect, that the statement is probable in relation to that evidence. In defending the statement, we may also submit it to further test. But testing is no substitute for justifying. After we have made our tests and added to the evidence at hand, we must weigh the evidence once again and ask whether, in the light of our new store of evidence, the statement we have tested is one which is itself acceptable or evident.[1]

The defense or justification of most of the statements we

---

[1] C. I. Lewis makes a similar distinction in *An Analysis of Knowledge and Valuation*, ch. ix. Compare John Ladd, *The Structure of a Moral Code* (Cambridge, Mass., 1957), ch. viii–ix; A. D. Woozley, "Knowing and Not Knowing," *Proceedings of the Aristotelian Society*, vol. LIII (1953); and Stephen Toulmin, "Probability," *ibid.*, suppl. vol. XXIV (1950).

make will refer, at least in part, to what we *perceive* or to what we *have* perceived. But our claims to perceive may themselves be challenged, and when they are, it is appropriate that we try to defend or to justify *them*. In the present chapter, I shall consider the way in which we do defend, or justify, our "perceptual claims." I shall try to make explicit what seems to be the characteristic "pattern" of such defense. We will then be in a position to consider two marks of evidence, two solutions to the problem of the criterion.

In this chapter and in the one that follows, I will not hesitate to attribute *evidence* to certain types of proposition or statement—propositions or statements which, I believe, most of us would agree to be evident. I shall attribute *evidence* to these propositions in the way in which a moral philosopher might attribute *rightness* to certain types of action. In the chapter following the next one, I shall consider what is involved in such attribution—what is meant, or conveyed, by the language in which it is expressed, and how we are to choose among conflicting theories of evidence.

2.   We may begin by considering a "perceptual claim" made in wholly ordinary circumstances.

Let us suppose that you say to me, as we are riding through New Hampshire, "I see that that is Mt. Monadnock behind the trees." If I should ask, "How do you know it's Monadnock?" you may reply by saying, "I've been here many times before and I can *see* that it is." If the matter happens to be of some importance and if I still have my doubts about what you claim to see, I will not ask you, of course, to defend or justify what you *see*. What you *see* is not the sort of thing that can be, or needs to be, justified; if you *do* see that it is Mt. Monadnock behind the trees, then you have all the justification you need for believing it is there. But I may ask, "What makes you *think* that's Monadnock that you see?" Or, using slightly different terms, I may ask, "What reason do you have for *taking* that to be Monadnock?" In the first case, I seem to be asking you to justify, not your perception of Mt. Monadnock, but your *belief* that you perceive it. In the second case, I seem to be asking you to justify another sort of act—your *taking* something to be Mt. Monadnock. But in either case the question calls for an inductive answer—an appeal to other statements in relation to which "That is Mt. Monadnock" may be said to be more probable than not.

An appropriate answer to my question would be this: "I can see that the mountain is shaped like a wave and that there is a little cabin near the top. There is no other mountain answering to that description within miles of here." What at first was justified merely by reference to perception ("I see that that is Mt. Monadnock") now seems to have the status of a hypothesis justified inductively by reference to a *different* perception. For what you now claim to see is, not that the mountain is Monadnock, but merely that it has a shape like a wave and that there is a cabin near the top. And this new "perceptual statement" is coupled with a statement of independent information ("Monadnock is shaped like a wave and there is a cabin near the top; no other mountain like that is within miles of here")—information acquired prior to the present perception. The new "perceptual statement" is considerably more modest than was the first.

If I remain unconvinced that Monadnock is the mountain you see, I may challenge (1) some one of your claims to independent information ("Why do you say that no other hills of that shape are near by?") or I may challenge (2) one of your new perceptual statements ("What makes you think you see a cabin near the top?"). If I take the second course, challenging your new perceptual statement, and if you continue to tolerate my questions, your reply, once again, is likely to consist of a new perceptual statement and a new claim to independent information. In defending your claim to see a *cabin*, perhaps you will say: "I see that it's more or less rectangular and that it's dark blue. I remember that there's such a cabin on Monadnock. It isn't probable that that thing could be anything else." (Or, at this point, instead of saying, "I see that . . . ," you may be more likely to say, "Don't you see that . . . ?").

We could say that the process we have been considering has a "pattern" or "form" like that of the following tree:

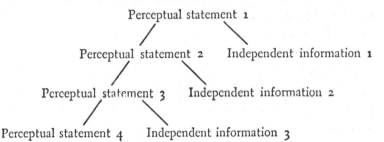

Perceptual statement 1

Perceptual statement 2   Independent information 1

Perceptual statement 3   Independent information 2

Perceptual statement 4   Independent information 3

I do not mean to suggest that such cross-examinations are likely to occur or to be tolerated. The point is, rather, that each perceptual statement of our example is one which, if it were defended, would be replaced by another perceptual statement and a statement purporting to express independent information.[2]

If we could continue the process of questioning and defending, thus adding lower branches to our tree, the contribution of perception might seem to become smaller. We would find the perceiver attributing more and more to information taken to be independently justified and less and less to his present perception. And we would reach a point where we find him making no *perceptual* claim at all.

---

[2] Compare Roderick Firth's description of "perceptual reduction" in "Sense-Data and the Percept Theory," *Mind*, LVIII (1949), especially 458 ff. See also A. M. Quinton, "The Problem of Perception," *Mind*, XLIV (1955), 28–51.

The question "What makes you say that the cabin is blue?" might not be tolerated in the circumstances of our example. And, if it were, the obvious reply would be: "Take a look for yourself!" But let us rule out the possibility of this reply, and let us assume that our perceiver is willing to co-operate. He will, then, reply in some such way as this: "Well, it *looks* blue from here. And if a thing that far away looks blue in this light then, in all probability, it *is* blue." When the perceiver replies in this way, he makes two claims once again: (1) he describes the way something appears and (2) he makes a generalization connecting such ways of appearing with certain characteristics of physical things. But he is no longer telling us what he *sees*.

We have been discussing the way in which a single perceptual claim—a claim to *see that* a certain state of affairs exists—might be defended. But the defense of any perceptual claim at all, whether it be a claim to see that a certain state of affairs exists, or to hear that one does, or to perceive by some other sense that it does, would exhibit a similar pattern. A perceiver, submitting to a similar cross-examination, would seem to replace his original perceptual claim by another, more modest perceptual claim; he would then replace the second by still another; and so on, until finally he makes no perceptual claim at all, but says something about what *appears*.

3. When our perceiver makes no perceptual statement, but refers instead to what appears, may we continue our cross-examination? What if we were to challenge his appear statement—"Well, it looks blue from here"—in the way we challenged his earlier perceptual statements?

In saying that something *looks* blue, our perceiver may mean to *compare* the thing he is looking at with other things—say, with lilacs, or the sky, or with a certain portion of the color chart. If this is what he intends, then his appear statement may be given a more explicit formulation. We noted, in the previous chapter, that "comparative" appear statements, of the form

x appears . . . to S

may be rendered in some such way as this:

x appears to S in the way in which things that are . . . might normally be expected to appear.

(Possibly the words "might normally be expected to appear" should be replaced; but this replacement would not affect any principle involved in what I am now trying to say.) If the statement "It looks blue from here" is to be taken in this comparative sense, then, like the statements above it on the left side of our tree, it is a statement whose defense would involve still *another* statement of independent information. The perceiver is now saying that there is a certain manner of appearing, f, which is such that (1) something now appears f and (2) things that are blue may normally be expected to appear f.

If we use the adjective "blue" where I have used the letter "f" just now, then "appears blue" should no longer be taken in its comparative sense. For the statement of independent information—"Things that are f (blue) may normally be expected to appear f (blue)"—is to be interpreted as a synthetic, nonlogical generalization. It does not say merely that things that are blue may normally be expected to appear in the way in which things that are blue may normally be expected to appear. It says, rather, that things that are blue may normally be expected to appear in the way in which (as it happens) this thing now appears. The expression "appears blue" now has what we have called its noncomparative use.

The second of our perceiver's two claims about appearing—his claim that things that are blue may normally be expected to look blue, in the noncomparative sense of "look blue"—is one which, once again, might be defended by an appeal to independent information, possibly by an appeal to what the perceiver remembers. He may recall that the sky, or lilacs, or a certain portion of the color chart usually appears in this particular way. But the *first* of his two claims about appearing, his claim that something now looks blue, does not depend upon this "independent" information. For even if this ostensible information is not information at all, even if the perceiver were mistaken with respect to what he thinks he remembers about the way in which lilacs and the sky and other blue things appear, it would not follow that he is mistaken in saying that something now looks *f*—that something now looks blue, in the noncomparative sense of "looks blue." And even if he were to modify his second claim, his appeal to independent information, saying merely, "This appears the way I *seem* to remember that blue things normally appear," the first claim is still distinct from the second. For what he now says, with respect to the manner of appearing, *f*, is (1) that something now appears *f* and (2) that he seems to remember that blue things ordinarily appear *f*.

Perhaps it is well to note that the statement expressing our perceiver's present claim—"Something now appears blue"—cannot be translated as "Something now appears in the way intended by my use of the expression 'appears blue.'" The latter statement, unlike the former, is a statement about language; to suppose that the one is a translation of the other is to confuse the *use* of language with the *mention* of language. Moreover, if there were reason to suppose that "Something now appears blue" is short for "Something now appears in the way intended by my use of the expression 'appears blue,'" then there would also be reason to suppose that the second of these sentences, in turn, is short for "Something now appears in the way intended by my use of the phrase 'intended by my use of the expression "appears blue,"'" and the new sentence, again, for "Something now appears in the way intended by my use of the phrase 'intended by my use of the phrase "intended by my use of the expression 'appears blue,' " ' " and so on. A similar objection applies to the thesis that "Something now appears blue" must, *in principle*, be comparative. It is sometimes supposed that every predicate is essentially comparative; that when we say something is *red*, for example, our intention is to *compare* that thing with some standard (possibly with what we remember as being red); and, more generally, that whenever we express ourselves in a statement of the form "*x* is *f*," our belief is one which could be more adequately expressed in a statement of the form "*x* is similar to the standard *f*." But if this thesis were true, then what is expressed by "*x* is similar to the standard *f*" would be even more adequately expressed by "*x* bears to the standard *f* a relation which is similar to the standard (first-order) similarity"; and so on.[3]

Returning now to our cross-examination, suppose we were to ask, "What makes you think something appears blue?" using the expression "appears blue" noncomparatively. What would be the point of this question?

It could be said, of a victim of hallucination, that although he is sensing an appearance, he is not sensing an appearance *of* anything.[4] Hence, if we ask, "What makes you think something appears blue?" we may mean to challenge our perceiver's claim that there is *something* which is appearing. If he were to accept our challenge and try to justify his assumption that he is not thus a victim of hallucination, he would refer again to his independent information—to information about conditions of observation and, possibly, about his own physiological or psy-

---

[3] Bertrand Russell has used this type of argument in a somewhat different connection; see *An Inquiry into Meaning and Truth* (New York, 1940), pp. 68–69, 345 ff.

[4] See Chapter Ten, Section 6.

chological state. In so doing, he would add another lower branch to the right side of our "tree." What of the left side of the tree? How would he formulate that more modest claim which now expresses his appeal to experience? If he were a philosopher, he might introduce a technical vocabulary. Another possibility would be to use the verb "appear" in the passive voice, saying, somewhat awkwardly, "I am appeared to blue," or "I am appeared to in a way which is blue." [5]

What, now, if we were to challenge our perceiver once again, asking, "What makes you think you are appeared to in a way which is blue?"

To *this* question, surely, the only appropriate reply—if any reply at all is appropriate—is "I just am." [6] Conceivably, our perceiver might provide additional information which would justify *us* in believing that he is "appeared blue to." But if he wished to describe *his own* justification for asserting the appear statement, he could do little more than to repeat his statement. [7] But this "defense by repetition" is never appropriate as a defense of a *perceptual* statement, a statement which could be prefixed by "I see that . . ." or "I perceive that . . ."

There is an important *epistemic* difference, then, between statements expressing our perceptual beliefs and some statements describing the ways in which we are "appeared to."

4.   There are two ways of describing the epistemic status of the "I am appeared to blue" of our example.

---

[5] In Chapters Eight and Ten, I shall elaborate upon the distinction between "*x* appears so-and-so to S" and "S is appeared to so-and-so." I shall propose that the active verb "to sense" be used in place of the passive form of "to appear."

[6] Compare Moritz Schlick, "Über das Fundament der Erkenntnis," *Erkenntnis*, IV (1934), 91, reprinted in *Gesammelte Aufsätze* (Vienna, 1938), p. 302. See also A. M. Quinton, *op. cit.*, p. 34 ff.

[7] If he were a philosopher, he might also make the point—to be discussed below—that "justification" may not be appropriate in this context.

Justification and Perception

We could say that our subject is *certain* of the truth of "I am appeared to blue" and that he is *not* certain of "The cabin on the hill is blue." In Chapter One, it may be recalled, I proposed to define "S is certain that h is true" by saying (i) that S knows that h is true and (ii) there is no i such that i is more worthy of S's belief than h. If we say that "I am appeared to blue" is *certain* for our subject, we mean that, for any other proposition, if he were forced to choose between that other proposition and "I am appeared to blue," he should *not* choose in favor of that other proposition. We could say, of the proposition attributed to perception—"The cabin on the hill is blue"— that, even though our perceiver may know it to be true, he is not certain of it, in the present sense of the word "certain." For if he *were* to find himself in a position where he had to choose between "The cabin on the hill is blue" and "I am now appeared to blue," he ought to choose the latter and reject the former. And he might find himself in such a position if he *were* to acquire adequate evidence for rejecting some of the statements expressing his "independent information"—if, say, he were to acquire adequate evidence for the hypothesis that, as a result of something he had eaten, only black things will appear blue to him. (An analogous situation is suggested if we consider a committee, appointed to elect several candidates. The committee may decide that Jones is a more acceptable candidate than is Smith and yet, quite consistently, also decide that both should be accepted. Their decision could be expressed this way: "As long as we don't have to choose between them, our decision that one is more acceptable than the other won't affect our choice. But if we *were* to find ourselves in a position where we had to accept one or the other and couldn't accept both, then—since Jones is the more acceptable of the two—we ought to accept Jones and reject Smith.") There are some philosophers, however, who would hesitate to say that "I am appeared to blue" is certain, or even that it is a statement which our perceiver *knows* to be true.

Hegel pointed out that a man is not worthy of being called "virtuous" unless he has known at least the temptation to sin; "virtue" is not appropriate in application to a state of pure innocence. Similarly, perhaps we should be reluctant to say that a man has attained a state of *knowledge,* or of *certainty,* unless he has at least run the risk of error. But, one could ask, where is the risk of error in the case of "I am now appeared to blue," when the statement is interpreted noncomparatively? Is it possible for me to be "appeared blue to" while I believe that I am not, or for me to believe that I am not "appeared blue to" at a time when I am? If we take "appear" in its *comparative* sense, then, of course, it *is* possible for me to be "appeared blue to" at a time when I do not believe that I am, and for me to believe that I am at a time when, in fact, I am not. For it may be that, because of unfamiliarity with things that are blue, I have a mistaken belief about the way in which blue things would ordinarily be expected to appear. But if "appear blue" is taken noncomparatively, then, surely, such mistakes cannot be made.[8] For *appearing blue,* in that sense, is one of

---

[8] Compare these remarks by C. S. Peirce (I think his term "percept" may be taken to mean the same as "appearance"): "If I judge a perceptual image to be red, I can conceive of another man's not having that same percept. I can also conceive of his having this percept but never having thought whether it was red or not. I can conceive that while colors are among his sensations, he shall never have had his attention directed to them. Or I can conceive that, instead of redness, a somewhat different conception should arise in his mind; that he should, for example, judge that this percept has a warmth of color. I can imagine that the redness of my percept is excessively faint and dim so that one can hardly make sure whether it is red or not. But that any man should have a percept similar to mine and should ask himself the question whether this percept be red, which would imply that he had already judged *some* percept to be red, and that he should, upon careful attention to this percept, pronounce it to be decidedly and clearly not red, when I judge it to be prominently

Justification and Perception

many ways of appearing which are such that, for any person at all, whenever that person is appeared to in one of those ways, it is false that he believes that he is *not* being appeared to in that particular way; and whenever he is not being appeared to in one of those ways, it is false that he believes that he *is* being appeared to in that particular way.

Hence if we do not say, of such statements as "I am now appeared to in a way which is blue," when intended noncomparatively, that they are *certain*, we should say, at least, that they are statements which cannot express any error or mistake. For if our perceiver cannot be said to believe, at a time when he is being "appeared blue to," that he is not being "appeared blue to," or to believe, at a time when he is not, that he is, then he cannot be said to believe erroneously or mistakenly at any time either that he is or that he is not being thus "appeared to." Perhaps we should say, more technically, that the appear statements in question are statements with respect to which it would "make no sense" to say that they can express any error or mistake.

We may also say of strings of nonsense syllables that they cannot express any error or mistake. But, epistemically, our appear statements differ from nonsense syllables in one very important respect: the appear statements, unlike any string of nonsense syllables, may be used as *premises* in the application of probability and, in certain contexts, therefore, may be taken

---

red, *that* I cannot comprehend at all. An abductive suggestion [that is, a "belief" in the ordinary sense of the word] is something whose truth *can* be questioned or even denied" (*Collected Papers* [Cambridge, Mass., 1934], 5.186). Compare Ludwig Wittgenstein, *Philosophical Investigations* (London, 1953), 89e, and Norman Malcolm, "Direct Perception," *Philosophical Quarterly*, III (1953), 301–316. An interesting historical discussion of the uses of epistemic terms in such contexts as the above is M. Chastaing, "Consciousness and Evidence," *Mind*, XLV (1956), 346–358.

Perceiving

as *evidence for* other statements or hypotheses. If our perceiver has adequate evidence for his hypothesis "Most of the things that look blue in this light are blue," if something now appears blue to him, and if he has no additional evidence bearing upon the thing that is now appearing blue to him, then he *also* has adequate evidence for the proposition that the thing he is looking at is something which is blue.

Using the locution "appears blue" in its noncomparative sense, let us say, therefore, that whenever any subject S is "appeared blue to," S has *adequate evidence* for the statement or hypothesis that he is thus being appeared to. And, more generally, whenever any subject is appeared to in one of the ways we have been talking about, then that subject has adequate evidence for the statement or hypothesis that he is being appeared to in that particular way.[9]

The *empirical criterion* of evidence, to which we now turn, refers to these ways of appearing. And *empiricism*, as an epistemic thesis, may be described as saying that the empirical criterion is the only criterion of evidence.

---

[9] There is, therefore, at least one respect in which each of us may be said to have "privileged access" to the ways in which we are appeared to. What serves for *me* as a mark of evidence that I am "appeared blue to" is the very fact that I *am* appeared blue to. But what serves for *you* as a mark of evidence for the proposition that I am "appeared blue to" is some *other* fact.

Six

On Some Marks of Evidence

1. We have said that a satisfactory criterion of evidence—a criterion for applying our locution "S has adequate evidence for h"—would refer to some *mark* of evidence. A mark, for any subject S, that S has adequate evidence for a given proposition or hypothesis h, would be, first, some state or condition of S which could be described without using "know," or "perceive," or "evident," or any other epistemic term. It would be, secondly, a state such that S could not be said to make any mistake at any time about his *being* in that state at that time. That is to say, S could never be said to believe falsely either that he is in that state or that he is not in that state. And a mark for S, that S has adequate evidence for a proposition or hypothesis h, would be, thirdly, a state or condition such that, whenever S is in that condition, S then has adequate evidence for h.

According to the *empirical criterion*, there are certain ways of "being appeared to" which can be described by using appear words noncomparatively and which are such that, whenever any subject S is "appeared to" in one of those ways, S then has

67

adequate evidence for the proposition that he is being appeared to in that particular way.

If what I have said in the previous chapter is accurate, then the empirical criterion provides us with a mark of evidence that fulfills our three conditions. First, the ways of "being appeared to" can be described without mentioning what the perceiver knows or has evidence for—without using any epistemic terms. Secondly, no one can ever be said to believe falsely either that he is being appeared to in one of those ways or that he isn't. We may say that, when a subject is thus appeared to, he is "certain" he is; or we may say that, when a subject is thus appeared to, it "makes no sense" to say that he believes that he is not being thus appeared to. Whichever way we put it, our second condition is fulfilled. And thirdly, whenever anyone is appeared to in one of those ways, he has adequate evidence for the proposition that he is being appeared to in that particular way.

We now have one criterion—the empirical criterion—for applying the locution "S has adequate evidence for *h*." The logic of probability, or confirmation, as we have noted in Chapter Two, tells us the conditions under which, given an application of "evidence" to a set of premises, we can apply it to still other propositions, statements, or hypotheses—hypotheses which are probable in relation to those premises. If our subject S has adequate evidence for a set of statements *h* about appearing, if, moreover, there are statements *i* which are *probable* in relation to those appearing statements *h*, and if, finally, S does not have adequate evidence for any statements in relation to which *i* is improbable, then S has adequate evidence for *i* as well as for *h*.

One of the philosophical theses of *empiricism* may now be formulated by reference to the empirical criterion of evidence and to the logic of probability, or confirmation.[1] According to

---

[1] I use the label "empiricism" in what I believe to be approximately its traditional sense, as intended, for example, in the expression "British

empiricism in its most extreme form, the empirical criterion, when supplemented by the logic of probability, affords us our *only* criterion of evidence. In other words, if a subject S has adequate evidence for a statement *h*, then either (a) *h* is a noncomparative statement describing the ways in which S is being appeared to or (b) *h* is a statement which is probable in relation to such noncomparative appear statements. Therefore, according to this extreme form of empiricism, if the perceiver discussed in the previous chapter has adequate evidence for saying, "That is Mt. Monadnock behind the trees," then the statement is one which is more probable than not in relation to statements describing, noncomparatively, the ways he is being appeared to.[2]

2. Empiricism resembles hedonism, or utilitarianism, in one significant respect. According to hedonism, or utilitarianism, in its most extreme form, the sole "right-making characteristics" are experiences of pleasure. According to empiricism, in its most extreme form, the sole "evidence-making characteristics" are certain ways of appearing. And although many philosophers have called themselves "hedonists," or "utilitarians," and many philosophers have called themselves "empiricists," few philosophers have been able to accept the extreme form of either view.

By concentrating on the left side of our "perceptual tree," as depicted in the previous chapter, we might be tempted to accept

---

empiricism," and not in its more recent sense, where it connotes a feeling about the importance of scientific method. The present *epistemic* thesis of empiricism must be distinguished from the *genetic* thesis I mentioned in Chapter Four, Sections 3 and 4; but the two theses are, of course, closely related.

[2] If the empirical criterion were our only criterion of evidence, we could say that the expression "*h* is probable in relation to the *total evidence* of S at *t*," which we used in Chapter Two, means: *h* is probable in relation to all of those purely noncomparative appear statements truly describing the way in which S is appeared to at *t*.

the thesis of empiricism. In defending or justifying our "claims to perceive," we may be led to make statements about the ways in which things appear. And these appear statements seem to be the "roots" of our tree. The uppermost perceptual claim is supported by a somewhat more modest perceptual claim; this more modest claim, in turn, is supported by another which is more modest still . . . ; and so on until we reach the roots of the tree where there are appear statements which are not, in the same sense, supported by anything at all. Changing the figure of speech slightly, we might say, as many philosophers have said, that such appear statements constitute the "basis" or "foundation" of the "structure of knowledge." [3] And—what may impress us even more—we may also say that, when such appear statements are used to defend those claims which at first had been defended by reference to *perception*, we no longer refer to perception at all. Perceiving, as a way of knowing, seems to have disappeared.

But is the empirical criterion our sole criterion of evidence?

The thesis of empiricism seems plausible when we restrict ourselves to the left side of our tree. But if we look at the other parts of the tree, we will recall that each time our perceiver defended

---

[3] Now, I think, we may be able to see the plausibility of the three genetic theses which, in Section 3 of Chapter Four, were also attributed to empiricism. For one who took the empirical criterion to be sufficient—to be our sole criterion of evidence—might well accept the three theses I there discussed. That is to say, he might well make statements of this sort: "Even if I don't know whether the apple I'm looking at is red, and even if, for some strange reason, I don't happen to know whether anything is red, I can at least be quite certain either that something now looks red to me or that nothing does. I never could know that an apple is red unless I knew either that it sometimes appears red or that something else, which I knew to be very much like the apple, sometimes appears red. The predicate 'red,' as it is intended in its ordinary use, may be defined in terms of 'appears red'; an apple may be said to 'be red' if and only if it appears red under optimum conditions." The appear words in these statements, it should be recalled, are to be taken noncomparatively.

a perceptual claim he appealed, not only to a more modest perceptual claim or to an appear statement, but *also* to a statement of "independent information," information presumably acquired at some earlier time. Indeed, we notice now that the perceptual claim at the top of our tree derives *most* of its support from this independent information—information which, so to speak, the perceiver brought with him to his present experience. The claim derives *some* support from the appear statement. But I shall suggest that, unless the appear statement is accompanied by some appeal to independent information, it will not support any of the perceptual claims above it.

Changing our figure of speech again, we might say, of the original perceptual claim ("That is Mt. Monadnock behind the trees"), that it is a horizontal structure supported by two posts or pillars—the one post being the appear statement and the other the appeal to independent information. If either post is removed and not replaced, the structure will collapse. To see that the appear statements are not enough to hold the structure, let us ask whether an ordinary "perceptual claim" can be said to be *probable*—more probable than not—in relation to any set of premises about "appearances."

To take as simple a case as possible, let us suppose that a man claims to see that something is blue. And let us suppose further that, in anwer to the kind of questioning I have attempted to illustrate, he declares finally: "Well, in the first place, the thing *looks* blue. And, in the second place, if the thing looks blue to me in this light, then, surely, it *is* blue." This reply is a good probability argument; if the man has adequate evidence for the premises, and if he is not leaving out anything that is relevant, then he has adequate evidence for his conclusion—his "perceptual claim" that the thing he is looking at is blue. But what if he were to omit the second premise, the premise saying that things which look blue in this light *are* blue? Can we say that the statement "The thing is blue" is probable in relation to the premise "The thing looks blue"?

This question has a strange sound because of the ambiguity of "looks." If I say, after examining all the evidence, "It looks as though we are going to have trouble in the spring," I mean that in all probability we shall have trouble in the spring. If "looks" is taken in this *epistemic* sense in "That looks blue," then it would be strange to ask whether "That is blue" is a statement which is probable in relation to "That looks blue." But we have described empiricism by reference to the *noncomparative* use of appear words, not by reference to their epistemic use. When we use "look" in this nonepistemic sense, there is nothing strange in saying, "I know that the thing is not blue, but this funny light makes it *look* blue." And there is nothing strange in asking whether "This is blue" is probable in relation to "This looks blue."

More often than not, of course, things which are blue do look blue—they do "present blue appearances." And, what is more important, things which look blue usually *are* blue. Knowing these facts, and knowing that something now looks blue, we can construct a good inductive argument for the conclusion that in all probability the thing that looks blue *is* blue. The premises of such an argument might include: (i) a statement about the frequency in which the characteristic of *being blue* occurs among the class of things that look blue; (ii) a statement about the frequency in which the characteristic of *looking blue* occurs among the class of things that are blue; and (iii) a statement saying of the sample at hand that it is one of the things that look blue. These premises—because of the frequencies which would be described in (i) and (ii)—would yield the conclusion (iv) that in all probability the sample is one of the things that are blue. The statement saying that the sample is blue is probable in relation to the three premises.

On Some Marks of Evidence

But this probability argument does not meet the requirements of what we have called "empiricism." If we are to meet these requirements—if we are to provide *empirical evidence* for the conclusion "That thing is blue"—our premises should refer only to the ways in which things, otherwise unspecified, happen to appear to us; our premises should not refer to any *other* characteristics of physical things.[4] But the premises of our present argument do not refer solely to the ways in which things appear. Premise (i) and premise (ii) refer to other characteristics of physical things; for they are generalizations about things which *are* blue.

Finding that something looks blue, we may also reason "from effect to cause" that the thing is blue. We know (i) that when something blue stimulates a "normal observer" under ordinary conditions the thing will "look blue" to him. If a man is looking at something blue, if his eyes and nervous system and brain are functioning as they are supposed to function, if there are no strange reflections, colored glasses, or the like, and if he sees the thing by daylight, then the thing will present him with "a blue appearance." And we may happen to know, of the present instance, (ii) that there are no strange lights or glasses, that the thing is seen in the light of day, and that our observer has no relevant disorders. Hence, once again, if we are given the "appearance" statement (iii) that something looks blue, we can reason, quite in accord with the logic of probability, (iv) that in all probability the thing which is appearing is something which is blue. But here, too, our premises are not confined to "appearance" statements; we are appealing, in (i) and (ii), to what we know about things which are blue and to what we know about the observer and the conditions of observation.

---

[4] More exactly: the premises should refer, not to the way in which something appears, but to the way in which the subject is "appeared to." The difference between these two locutions will be discussed in Chapter Ten.

What we set out to find was a probability argument whose premises are statements which refer to "appearances" and which do not express information about any characteristic other than that of "appearing" or "looking." But if our conclusion is to state that, in all probability, a certain thing *is* blue, then, I believe, we cannot find such an argument. Whether we reason from effect to cause or from cause to effect, from sample to population, from population to sample, or from one sample of a certain population to another sample of that same population, any argument concluding that something probably *is* blue will contain some premise expressing information about a characteristic *other* than that of "appearing" or "looking"; that is to say, the premises will include some synthetic statement which is not an "appearance" statement. Using such premises, many philosophers have constructed "proofs" of the external world. But no one, I believe, has ever constructed a good inductive argument whose premises contain only appear statements of the sort we have been discussing and whose conclusion ascribes, to some "external" physical thing, any characteristic other than that of appearing in some way.

The empirical criterion, therefore, has been closely associated with skepticism. Hume said that "in all our reasonings" we should take for granted that "it is in vain to ask, whether there be body or not?" [5] And he was led to say this because he thought that the thesis of empiricism is one of the principles we should take for granted in all our reasonings. It was undoubtedly a similar thought which led Kant to say that our inability to prove "the existence of things outside us" is a "scandal to philosophy and to human reason in general." [6]

---

[5] *Treatise of Human Nature,* bk. I, pt. IV, sec. 2 ("Of Scepticism with Regard to the Senses").

[6] *The Critique of Pure Reason,* B xxxix; Norman Kemp Smith ed. (London, 1933), p. 34.

On Some Marks of Evidence

One may ask, as Kant and Hume had asked: "*If* we are confined to premises which describe 'appearances' or 'sensations,' what justification do we have for our beliefs about 'external physical things'?" On hearing a question which is put in this way, perhaps we tend to assume that the antecedent is true. A comparable question, however, is this one: "*If* we are confined to premises describing only what occurs at the present time, what justification do we have for accepting any conclusion which tells about what has happened in the past?" The two hypothetical questions may be answered alike. Under the conditions set by the antecedents, we would not have adequate evidence for the beliefs described in the consequents. But this fact does not warrant skepticism and despair. For our answers to these hypothetical questions are not problems for us unless we have accepted the conditions set by the antecedents.

"A traveler of good judgment," Thomas Reid has said in this connection, "may mistake his way, and be unawares led into a wrong track; and while the road is fair before him, he may go on without suspicion and be followed by others; but when it ends in a coal-pit, it requires no great judgment to know that he hath gone wrong, nor perhaps to find out what misled him." [7]

To find the right road, we must find some other criteria of evidence.

3. According to the definition proposed in Chapter One, the locution "S *perceives* something to have such and such a characteristic" means: there is something which has such and such a characteristic and which appears in some way to S; S *takes* the thing to have that characteristic; and he has adequate evidence for the hypothesis that the thing does have that characteristic.

---

[7] *An Inquiry into the Human Mind,* ch. i, sec. 8. "Phenomenalism" is a view which, if it were true, might provide the empiricist with a way of avoiding the coalpit. I shall discuss this view critically in the Appendix

"Taking," in the sense in which it is intended here, is related to "perceiving" in the way in which "accepting," or "believing," is related to "knowing." (See Chapter One, Section 6.) I suggest that this concept of *taking* will lead us to another mark of evidence.

Wittgenstein remarked that "one doesn't '*take*' what one knows as the cutlery at a meal *for* cutlery; any more than one ordinarily tries to move one's mouth as one eats, or aims at moving it." [8] And it is doubtless true that if I *see*—if I *perceive* —that it's cutlery, I wouldn't *say*, "I take it to be cutlery." I'm not likely to *say*, "I take it to be cutlery" unless I feel some doubt or hesitation.[9] But this fact must not be taken to mean that "I see that it's cutlery" implies "It's false that I take it to be cutlery." [10] Another guest trying to make up his own mind may say of me, "Well, *he* takes it to be cutlery," without intending to imply that I do *not* see or perceive that it is. On learning that the King is dead, his subjects do not *say*, "Some man has passed away"; but "The King is dead" *entails* "Some man has passed away."

If a man were to say, "I perceive—I see—that there is a cat on the roof," and if we thought him to be in error, we could ask, "But why do you *take* that thing to be a cat?" And if he were to decide, at some later time, that he was in error, he might well say, "I thought I saw a cat—I *took* something to be a cat—but I was mistaken."

Let us try to formulate a definition of *taking* which will be adequate to the use of "take" in our definition, above, of the

---

[8] *Philosophical Investigations*, p. 195e.

[9] Compare Cardinal Newman: "Whatever a man holds to be true, he will say he holds for certain" (*A Grammar of Assent* [London, 1913], p. 197).

[10] "It's false that I take it to be cutlery" must be distinguished in meaning from "I don't take it to be cutlery," for the latter sentence is usually intended to mean the same as "I take it *not* to be cutlery."

On Some Marks of Evidence

propositional use of "perceive" and which will enable us to say that, in certain instances, *taking* is a mark of evidence. I suggest this definition:

"S *takes* something x to be f" means: S believes (i) that x's being f is a causal condition of the way he is being appeared to and (ii) that there are possible ways of varying x which would cause concomitant variations in the way he is appeared to.

If our perceiver takes something to be a cat, then he believes that a cat is one of the causes of the way he is appeared to.[11] And he believes further that by "varying" the cat in suitable ways—for example, by moving it—he could produce concomitant variations in the way he is appeared to. "Believe" is here intended in the broad sense in which it was introduced in Chapter One (Section 6). He may not *think* of such variations but he would be very surprised if they were *not* to occur.

Our definition, it should be emphasized, does not say that taking is a kind of *inferring*. Our perceiver need not have "framed a hypothesis" about the causal conditions of the way in which he was appeared to. His belief may have been wholly spontaneous and thus not acquired as the result of reflection, deliberation, or inference.[12]

---

[11] Why not say merely, "He believes a cat is appearing to him"? In Chapter Ten, I shall define the locution "x appears so-and-so to S" by reference to certain concepts of physics and physiology; hence, if we were to define "take" in terms of "x appears," we would have to say, implausibly, that no one can take anything to be a cat unless he has a certain belief involving these concepts.

[12] In Chapter Ten, I shall relate this definition to what is sometimes described as "the causal theory of perception." It should be noted that, in one of its ordinary senses—but not in the sense intended here—"taking" is a synonym for "inferring." Compare: "From the reports I have read, I take it that there may still be some liberals in Czechoslovakia."

Perceiving

May we say that *taking*, as defined, provides us with a mark of evidence?

I believe we have been able to say what *taking* is without using any epistemic terms. In saying what it is for a man to take something to be a cat, we have not used such words as "know," "evident," "see," or "perceive." Hence, if our description is accurate, *taking* meets the first of our three conditions.

No one can be said ever to believe falsely, or mistakenly, either that he is taking something to be a cat or that he is not taking something to be a cat. A man may take something, falsely, to be a cat; that is to say, he may *mis*take something for a cat. And conceivably a man may believe falsely today that yesterday he took something to be a cat. But a man cannot *now* believe falsely that he is *now* taking something to be one, or that he is *not* now taking something to be one. We may say that he is "certain" that he is taking something to be a cat—or we may say "it makes no sense" to say he believes falsely he is taking something to be one. But whichever locution we use—"he is certain" or "it makes no sense"—it will follow that he cannot be said to believe falsely that he is taking something to be one. And we can say, more generally, with respect to any subject S, that S can never be said to believe falsely at any time either that he is or that he is not taking something at that time to have a certain characteristic. Hence *taking* meets our second condition.

Does *taking* meet our third condition? Do we wish to say that, whenever a man *takes* something to have a certain characteristic, he thereby has adequate evidence for believing that the thing *has* that characteristic?

It is obvious, I think, that whenever a man takes something to have a certain characteristic he then has adequate evidence for the proposition that he *does* take the thing to have that characteristic. In this respect, *taking* is like many other attitudes.

On Some Marks of Evidence

For example, if a man *believes* that there is music on the piano, then he has evidence for the proposition that he *does* believe that there is music on the piano.[13] But, according to the proposed criterion we are now discussing, taking provides evidence, not only for itself, but also for its object: if S takes x to be f, S has adequate evidence for the proposition that S does take x to be f and *also* for the proposition that x is f.

Given this criterion of evidence, we need no longer say that "it is in vain to ask whether there be body." We have only to say what we now take to be true, what we think we perceive, and we will thereby have indicated a large number of propositions for which we have adequate evidence and which describe in detail the "external" things around us. Hence we avoid the skeptical consequences to which the empirical criterion seemed to lead us.

But our present criterion leads us to another undesirable extreme.

If a spectator feels certain that the defendant is the man who is guilty, then, if he takes someone in the courtroom to be the defendant, he will, thereby, also take him to be the man who is guilty. For he will believe, with respect to the way he is "appeared to," that he wouldn't be appeared to in that way under those conditions if the defendant—the man he believes to be guilty—were not there. Hence, the proposed criterion of evidence implies that, in such a case, the spectator has adequate evidence for believing the defendant guilty. Again: if a man believes, however unreasonably, that most of the people who work on the docks are Communists, and that most Communists

---

[13] The term "self-evident" is appropriate in these cases inasmuch as the occurrence of the mark of evidence is evidence for itself; "the evidenced item is strictly identical with the evidencing item." The quotation is from C. J. Ducasse, "Propositions, Truth and the Ultimate Criterion of Truth," *Philosophy and Phenomenological Research*, IV (1944), 338.

are untrustworthy, and if he has accepted the rumor that his neighbor's brother works on the docks, then it may be that, in taking someone to be his neighbor's brother, he will also take that person to be untrustworthy. For he will believe, with respect to the ways he is being "appeared to," that he wouldn't be appeared to in those ways unless the person in question were his neighbor's brother and, therefore, someone who is untrustworthy. The "taking" criterion of evidence would require us to say that, in such a case, our perceiver has adequate evidence for the proposition that the man he is looking at *is* untrustworthy.[14]

Where the empirical criterion does not seem to allow us enough evidence, the "taking" criterion, in its present form, seems to allow us too much. Hence we must try to formulate a compromise criterion—to find another mark of evidence—which will enable us to avoid these extremes of defect and excess.

4. Any satisfactory criterion, I am afraid, will be considerably more complex than either empiricism or the "taking" criterion. And we cannot be certain that we have a satisfactory criterion—that our criterion is neither excessive nor defective with respect to the evidence it allows—unless we make use of the logic of confirmation, or probability, and give our subject a much more rigorous treatment than I am capable of giving it. But I shall attempt to say what a satisfactory criterion would be like. And I shall discuss some of the philosophical problems which the acceptance of any such criterion seems to involve.

The plausibility of empiricism derives partly from the fact that the marks of evidence to which it appeals may be found

---

[14] In a symposium on "The Concept of Evidence," held at the meeting of the Eastern Division of the American Philosophical Association at the University of Pennsylvania, December 28, 1956, Richard Brandt noted that the "taking" criterion has this type of defect.

only at the lowest level—at the "roots"—of our "perceptual tree." The implausibility of the " taking" criterion derives partly from the fact that the marks of evidence to which it appeals may be found at any level of our tree. We will not find an acceptable compromise, I believe, unless we consider some of the other parts of the tree.

The perceiver who served to illustrate our tree had begun, it may be recalled, by saying:

(1) I see that that is Mt. Monadnock behind the trees.

After being questioned ("But why do you say it's Mt. Monadnock that you see?"), he referred to certain independent information about Mt. Monadnock, including the fact that there is a cabin near the top, and he then made a more modest claim which may be expressed in this way:

(2) I see that there is a cabin near the top.

When this claim was challenged, he referred again to his independent information, including the fact that the cabin is blue. We may formulate his next claim this way:

(3) I see that there is something there which is blue.

On further questioning, he said, in effect:

(4) There is something that appears to me in the way in which blue things would appear under conditions like these.

But he had expressed (4) by saying "It looks blue from here," using the locution "looks blue" in what I have called its comparative sense. He was then led to defend the reference to blue things by appeal, once again, to independent information. But he could still say:

(5) There is something that appears blue to me

now using "appears blue" in what I have called its noncomparative sense. And finally, after considering the possibility of hallucination and excluding that possibility by reference to independent information, he said in effect:

(6) I am appeared to in a way which is blue.

According to the empirical criterion of evidence, such statements as (1) through (5) are not evident unless they are probable in relation to such statements as (6), occurring at the lowest level of our tree. But according to the "taking" criterion, statements (1) through (3), at the top of our tree, are evident provided only that they do, in fact, express what our perceiver believes. Our compromise criterion, I suggest, should not include (1) and (2); that is to say, the mere fact that our perceiver *takes* something to be Monadnock, or *takes* something to be a cabin, does not guarantee that he has adequate evidence for the proposition he takes to be true. But our criterion should include more than (6); there are statements for which our perceiver has adequate evidence but which may not be probable in relation to such statements as (6).

I suggest that statement (3)—"I see that there is something which is blue"— is a statement for which our perceiver has adequate evidence, provided only it expresses what he believes. In other words, if he *takes* something to be blue, then he has adequate evidence for the proposition that that thing is blue— even if the proposition is false and even if nothing whatever is appearing to him. I suggest, more generally, that (3) exemplifies a certain class of *takings,* all of which constitute marks of evidence.

The following quotation from Price's *Perception* refers to the class of *takings* I have in mind and, I believe, indicates the type of criterion we need.

We want to be able to say: the fact that a material thing is perceptually presented to the mind is *prima facie evidence* of the thing's

On Some Marks of Evidence

existence and of its really having that sort of surface which it ostensibly has; or, again, that there is *some presumption in favour of* this, not merely in the sense that we do as a matter of fact presume it (which of course we do) but in the sense that we are entitled to do so. But what exactly must the presumption be in favour of, and what is to be *prima facie* evidence for what? Clearly we shall have to say that the existence of a particular visual or tactual sense-datum is *prima facie* evidence (1) for the existence of a material thing such that this sense-datum belongs to it, (2) for the general possession by this thing of a front surface of a certain general sort. The proposition may be called the *Principle of Confirmability;* for unless it were true, no confirmation of a perceptual act by other perceptual acts would ever be possible.[15]

I shall attempt to formulate a similar criterion by reference to a certain class of characteristics and relations. The characteristics include: being *blue, red, green,* or *yellow;* being *hard, soft, rough, smooth, heavy, light, hot,* or *cold;* and that of *sounding,* or *making-a-noise.* The relations include: being the *same,* or *different,* with respect to any of the characteristics in question; being *more like* one object than another with respect to any of the characteristics, or with respect to hue, saturation, and brightness, or with respect to loudness, pitch, and timbre. The class of characteristics and relations also includes the "common sensibles"—that is, "movement, rest, number, figure, magnitude"— as well as what is intended by such terms as "above," "below," "right," "left," "near," "far," "next," "before," "after," "simultaneous," and "to last" or "to endure." In short, the characteristics and relations in question are coextensive with what Aristotelians have traditionally referred to as the "proper objects of sense" and the "common sensibles" and with what Reid described as the objects of "original" perception.[16] Let us use the

---

[15] H. H. Price, *Perception* (London, 1932), p. 185.
[16] See Aristotle, *De Anima,* 425a–427b. In *An Inquiry into the Human*

word "sensible" in a somewhat restricted sense and refer to these characteristics and relations as *sensible* characteristics and relations.

We may now consider the following criterion—or group of criteria.

(a) Whenever we *take* something to have, or not to have, a certain sensible characteristic, or whenever we take a group of things to stand, or not to stand, in a certain sensible relation, we then have adequate evidence for the propositions we thus take to be true.

(b) Whenever we take something, which we believe to be appearing to us in one way, to be the same as, or to be different from, something we believe to be appearing to us in another way, we then have adequate evidence for the propositions we thus take to be true. If I take the thing I think I'm hearing to be the same as the thing I think I'm seeing, then I have adequate evidence for the proposition that they are the same.

(c) Our criterion should also include the original empirical criterion: any belief, expressible in a noncomparative statement describing the ways in which we are appeared to, is a belief for which we have adequate evidence.

(d) And, finally, we should add a reference to beliefs con-

Mind (ch. vi, sec. 20), Thomas Reid said: "Our perceptions are of two kinds: some are natural and original; others acquired and the fruit of experience. When I perceive that this is the taste of cider, that of brandy; that this is the smell of an apple, that of an orange; that this is the noise of thunder, that the ringing of bells; this the sound of a coach passing, that the voice of such a friend: these perceptions, and others of the same kind, are not original—they are acquired. But the perception which I have, by touch, of the hardness and softness of bodies, of their extension, figure, and motion, is not acquired—it is original." Reid adds that, by sight "we perceive originally the visible figure and colour of bodies only, and their visible place." In saying above that the class of *sensible* characteristics and relations are those to which Reid's theory of "original perception" pertains, I do not thereby commit myself to Reid's psychological theories about "original" and "acquired" perception.

cerning the similarities and differences among ways of appearing: whenever we believe, with respect to any of the ways in which we believe things x, y, and z are appearing to us, that x is the same as (or different from) y, or that x is more like y than like z, then we have adequate evidence for the propositions that, with respect to those ways of appearing, there is something x which is the same as (or different from) something y, or that there are things x, y, and z such that, with respect to those ways of appearing, x is more like y than like z. The ways of appearing in question are, once again, those which are describable in noncomparative appear statements.[17]

We may express our compromise criterion briefly by saying that, according to it, we have evidence for all of our *sensible takings*.[18]

Our compromise avoids the extremes of empiricism and of the unqualified "taking" criterion. I believe that it satisfies the first two of the three conditions which, we said, any criterion of evidence should meet. For the class of *sensible takings* has been described without the use of epistemic terms; and, I believe, it is impossible for anyone to believe falsely, with respect to any sensible characteristic or relation, that he is (or that he

---

[17] I did not include olfactory and gustatory characteristics in the list of sensible characteristics. But (d) allows us to say that we have evidence for such statements as "This smells sweeter than that does" and "This tastes more bitter than that," where "smells sweet" and "tastes bitter" are noncomparative appear expressions. It should be recalled that, when I say that the locution "x appears so-and-so" is *noncomparative*, I mean, in part, that "x appears so-and-so" does not entail any such locution as "x appears in the way in which things that are so-and-so appear under such-and-such conditions." Statements may be noncomparative in this sense and yet make the kind of comparisons referred to in (d).

[18] If we were to accept this criterion, and only this one, we could reformulate the definition of "h is probable in relation to the *total evidence* of S at t" so that the locution could be said to mean: h is probable in relation to all of those propositions which, at t, S sensibly takes to be true.

isn't) taking something to have that characteristic or to stand in that relation. But we do not yet know whether the road is fair before us.

5. The way in which we defend our "sensible takings" may suggest an objection to our attempt at a compromise criterion. Whenever a man defends one of his "takings," sensible or otherwise, he appeals, in part, to independent information—to what he remembers, or thinks he remembers. If you challenge one of my "sensible takings," asking, say, "Why do you take that to be *blue?*" and if I take your question seriously, I will reply by making two assertions. Perhaps I will say, (a) "It looks—appears—blue" and (b) "For the most part, whatever looks blue under these conditions *is* blue." In the present context, as we have seen, the second of these statements is synthetic, expressing information independently acquired. It should not be supposed however, that in replacing my original statement—"I take that to be blue"—by the two statements constituting its defense, I have thereby *revoked* the original statement. Since you did not see the need to accept the original claim, I offered you other premises—premises which I thought you would be more likely to accept and in relation to which the original claim could be seen to be probable.[19]

Some of our "sensible takings" may be more probable, in relation to the rest of our knowledge, or to the rest of our evident

---

[19] It is quite likely that in the instance under consideration I would not have made the claim had I not recalled the "independent information" expressed in (b) above—the information that, in conditions like those I now believe to hold, most of the things that look blue *are* blue. We should not assume, however, that taking is always a function of remembering; we should not assume that before one can *take* some proposition to be true, one must first be able to *remember* some closely related proposition to be true. I shall discuss an alternative to this assumption in Chapter Nine, Section 4.

On Some Marks of Evidence

beliefs, than are others. And many of them are false, or mistaken. What we "take" will depend upon what we already believe, and if what we believe is false, the "takings" may be false. Looking at a car that is blue and not knowing the effects of the arc lights above it, a man may take it to be green. Our "takings"—sensible and otherwise—are notoriously affected by our emotions, attitudes, and wishes. A hunter may take a cat, or a stone, to have the shape and size of a rabbit; a hungry man, on looking at the word "fool," may take it to be "food"; an amateur proofreader may take a misspelled word to have the shapes it would have if the spelling were correct. But even if a man's "sensible takings" are the result of systematic delusion or hallucination, or the result of some defect of his sense organs or his brain, these "takings," according to my suggestion, are a mark of evidence. If our friend takes the blue car to be green, then he has adequate evidence for the proposition or statement that what is before him *is* green. But *we* may know that he is mistaken.

Scholastic philosophers speak about *objective evidence*, evidence which is "entirely caused and imposed by the object" and which is thus "safe from any danger of illusion, confusion, or distortion." [20] If we could find a subclass of "taking"—or of "sensible taking"—which is objective in this sense, our criterion of evidence might seem more acceptable. For we could then say: "sensible taking" is a source of evidence provided that the "taking" is objective, provided that it is caused only by the object and is thus safe from illusion, confusion, and distortion. But unfortunately there are no such "takings." Every instance of "taking" is a result both of external stimulation and of the psychological and physiological state of the perceiver.

Some of our "sensible takings," to be sure, are *not* the re-

---

[20] See Fernand von Steenberghen, *Epistemology* (New York, 1949), p. 195.

sult of organic defects, or of prior mistakes, or of illusion and distortion. Our sense organs do sometimes work properly, and not all of the beliefs we bring with us to experience are false or unreasonable. One might wish to say, therefore, that only these good "takings" are a source of evidence. But if we say this, our criterion no longer meets the second of our requirements. Our mark of evidence must be a state or condition such that a man can never be said to believe falsely that he is in that state, or to believe falsely that he is not in that state. A man *can* believe falsely, however, that his "taking" is a good "taking"; he may well believe falsely that his present "taking" is not the result of an organic defect or of a mistake.

A problem which is even more serious is suggested by this possibility: suppose there is a man who believes that all and only blue things are cold.[21] It may be that whenever he takes anything to have the sensible quality blue he also takes it to have the sensible quality cold. Hence we may have to say that whenever he sees that something is blue, then, no matter what the thing may be, he also has adequate evidence for the hypothesis that it is cold. But I think we may accept this consequence.

The apparent paradox involved in saying that the false "sensible takings"—the *mistakes*—are a mark of evidence has its analogue in moral philosophy. We noted in Chapter One that it is difficult to avoid saying that occasionally the *right* choice has consequences that are worse than those the *wrong* choice would have had—or that the wrong choice has consequences better than those the right choice would have had. A man who gives up his life jacket with the intention of sacrificing himself and saving others may be doing what is right, even though, as a result of his act, he alone is saved. (But if, in so doing, he were acting upon an unreasonable hypothesis, we might well

---

[21] This example was suggested to me by Mr. Timothy Duggan.

condemn him for his judgment.) Most of us would accept the apparent ethical paradox on the ground that the alternative views are even more paradoxical. I would defend our epistemic view on similar grounds.

Our criterion, moreover, may have the kind of "internal" justification we discussed in Chapter Three (Section 3). For I believe that the hypotheses and propositions which *are* evident on this criterion indicate that most of our "sensible takings" are true—that most of them are *perceivings*. These hypotheses and propositions, as Peirce noted, indicate that human beings have a tendency to make correct guesses and that the human mind is "strongly adapted to the comprehension of the world." [22] In other words, I think we can inductively confirm the hypothesis that those "sensible takings" we have called marks of evidence are also marks of *truth*. We know that any false belief about the association of sensible qualities will not long survive; if there is a man who believes that all blue things are cold and all cold things are blue, then, sooner or later, experience will "filter off" these false ideas, "eliminating them and letting the truth pour on in its mighty current." [23]

We sometimes use the adverbs "really," "strictly," and "literally" in such a way that a man can be said *really, strictly,* or *literally* to perceive some *x* to be *f* only if *f* is some sensible characteristic or relation. A witness may be led to concede that what he "really" saw—what he "strictly" or "literally" saw—was, not that the defendant was carrying a gun, but rather that he was carrying something *shaped* like a gun, or shaped

---

[22] *Collected Papers*, 6.417. "This calls to mind one of the most wonderful features of reasoning and one of the most important philosophemes in the doctrine of science, of which, however, you will search in vain for any mention in any book I can think of; namely, that reasoning tends to correct itself, and the more so, the more wisely its plan is laid. Nay, it not only corrects its conclusions, it even corrects its premisses" (5.575).

[23] *Ibid.*, 5.50.

in the way he remembers a gun to be shaped. And philosophers may tell us that, when we claim to see our family at the table before us, what we *really* see is, at most, that there is a collection of things before us having certain colors and shapes and related to each other in certain spatial and other sensible ways. There is no need to object to this manner of speaking, provided we realize that "really," "strictly," and "literally," in this use, function as synonyms for our term "sensibly." [24] But we may also say that the witness *did* see the defendant to be carrying a gun, that we *do* see our family at the table before us, and that our original perceiver *did* see that his cat was on the roof—provided that, in each case, the proposition which is thus taken to be true is a true proposition for which the perceiver has adequate evidence. And if the proposition is one for which he has adequate evidence, then it is one which is probable in relation to the conjunction of his present "sensible taking" with what he claims to remember.

6. I have said, in effect, that if a man *thinks he perceives* a thing to have certain sensible characteristics, he thereby has adequate evidence for believing that the thing has those characteristics. We should also say, I believe, that if a man *thinks he remembers* taking something to have had such characteris-

---

[24] And provided we know when *not* to ask, "But what did you *really* perceive?" If we put this question to someone who has made an ordinary perceptual claim, if we put it again after we have received an answer, and if we continue in this way, we arrive at the "perceptual tree" of the previous chapter. But when our perceiver has reached the lower parts of the tree and refers only to the sensible characteristics he claims to perceive, it is no longer appropriate to ask, "But what did you really perceive?" The peculiar philosophical view, that appearances or ways of appearing are what we really perceive, often results, as H. A. Prichard pointed out, "from our having put the question 'What do we really see?' just once too often" (*Knowledge and Perception* [Oxford, 1950], p. 58). I shall discuss this philosophical view in Chapter Ten, Section 4.

tics he thereby has adequate evidence for believing that it had them.[25]

Whenever we think we remember a certain event to have occurred, we will say that we *do* remember that event to have occurred. And it is impossible, of course, for a man to be mistaken in what he does remember—we cannot remember mistakenly any more than we can perceive or know mistakenly. But we often make mistakes with respect to what we *think* we perceive or know, and so, too, we often make mistakes with respect to what we think we remember. "I thought I remembered seeing him at the meeting, but I realize now it couldn't have been he.[26]

Thinking that one remembers, I suggest, provides still another mark of evidence. If we were attempting to present a complete theory of evidence, it would be necessary to describe this mark without using the epistemic term "remember," and therefore without using the expression "thinking that one remembers." The kind of spontaneous assurance about the past

---

[25] To say this is not to deny Gilbert Ryle's principle that "though 'recall' is a 'got it' verb, it is not a verb of finding, solving or proving" (*The Concept of Mind*, p. 278). What we *have* when we recall, or think we recall, is adequate evidence. But we don't *infer* that, *because* we have recalled so-and-so, we therefore have adequate evidence that so-and-so.

[26] There are some terminological problems involved in describing mistakes of memory, or, rather, mistakes with respect to what one thinks one remembers. Suppose that, at yesterday's meeting, I *mistook* another man for you, thus thinking it was you that I saw. Should we say that today's statement "I remember seeing you at the meeting" expresses a mistake of memory? Memory isn't to blame in this case; but the memory statement, strictly interpreted, is false, since it implies the false statement "I saw you yesterday." In other cases, of course, memory—the process of thinking that one remembers—*is* to blame. One may say, for example: "I thought I remembered seeing you at the meeting; but now I remember it wasn't you I was thinking of—I didn't see you there." G. E. M. Anscombe mentions the first type of case in "The Reality of the Past," in Max Black, ed., *Philosophical Analysis* (Ithaca, N.Y., 1950), pp. 44–45.

that is essential to "thinking that one remembers" can be described, I believe, without using any epistemic terms, but I shall not attempt such a description here.

Thinking that one remembers is like believing, taking, questioning, and other such attitudes, in that it "provides evidence for itself": if a man thinks he remembers a certain proposition to be true, then he has adequate evidence for believing that he *does* think he remembers that proposition to be true. Moreover, according to what I have just suggested, thinking-that-one-remembers is, in certain instances, like sensibly-taking, in that it also provides evidence for its object. If I now think I remember that something had a certain sensible characteristic or that a group of objects stood in certain sensible relations, then I have adequate evidence for believing the propositions which I thus think I remember. If I now think I remember that I believed, took, or thought I remembered a certain proposition to be true, then I have adequate evidence for believing that I did believe, take, or think I remembered that proposition to be true. And if I now think I remember having been "appeared to" in a certain way, then I have adequate evidence for believing that I was appeared to in that way.[27]

Some philosophers have suggested a more liberal view of the evidence that is supplied by thinking-that-one-remembers.

---

[27] We should also have a memory principle comparable to (d) in our formulation of the "sensibly-taking" criterion. For instance, we should say this: whenever we believe, with respect to any of the ways in which we believe something x to be appearing to us, and with respect to one of the ways in which we think we remember that something y did appear to us, that x is the same as (or different from) y, then we have adequate evidence for the proposition that there is now something x and there was once something y such that, with respect to those ways of appearing, x is the same as (or different from) y; and so on. And perhaps we should add a similar principle for the case where *both* x and y are things we think-we-remember to have appeared to us.

On Some Marks of Evidence

They have suggested that *whenever* one thinks one remembers a certain proposition to be true one thereby has adequate evidence for believing that proposition to be true.[28] If I now think I remember having seen the *Andrea Doria* when it first arrived in New York, then, according to the view in question, I have adequate evidence for believing I did see the *Andrea Doria* when it first arrived in New York. This liberal view, I believe, has consequences like those which led us to reject the unqualified "taking" criterion above. Let us recall our example about the man who believes, unreasonably, that most of the people who work along the docks are Communists, that most Communists are dishonest, and that his neighbor's brother works along the docks. In taking someone to be his neighbor's brother, he took that person to be someone who is dishonest. Today he thinks he remembers seeing the man; he also thinks he remembers seeing someone who is dishonest. ("There was money stolen from the cashier's desk? I remember seeing a dishonest man near by.") [29] Hence if thinking-that-one-remembers provides one with a mark of evidence for the proposition thought

---

[28] In *An Analysis of Knowledge and Valuation*, C. I. Lewis defends the principle that "whatever is [thought to be] remembered, whether as explicit recollection or merely in the form of our sense of the past, is *prima facie* credible because so remembered." But he adds this second principle: "When the whole range of empirical beliefs is taken into account, all of them more or less dependent upon memorial knowledge, we find that those which are most credible can be assured by their mutual support, or as we shall put it, their *congruence*" (p. 334).

[29] I think there may be those who would say: even if the person of our example *were* dishonest, what our perceiver remembers seeing—in the "real," "strict," or "literal" sense of "remember"—is, *not* that there was a dishonest man standing near by, but merely that there was something before him having such-and-such sensible characteristics. This "literal" use of "remember"—if indeed there is such a use—is closely related to what we have described as the "literal" use of "perceive": we "literally remember" only those propositions we have "literally perceived" (or taken?) to be true.

to be remembered, we must say once again that our perceiver has adequate evidence for the proposition that he saw someone dishonest.

Can we avoid the "coalpit" of empiricism merely by supplementing the empirical criterion with some version of the "thinking-that-one-remembers" criterion? I think that this set of criteria—"being appeared to" plus "thinking that one remembers"—might yield some paradoxical consequences. For example, it might require us to say that, although (a) at the time I take something to be red I may not have adequate evidence for the proposition that the thing is red, nevertheless (b) I will have adequate evidence for this proposition at a *later* date provided only that I then think I remember having taken the thing, at the earlier date, to be red. But the question whether these criteria would lead us out of the coalpit is a technical question. To answer it we would need to examine the results of applying the logic of confirmation to what, on these criteria, would be our "total evidence"—to all of those statements describing the way we are appeared to at any given time and describing what (in the desired sense) we think we remember at that time.[30]

7. The philosopher may attempt to formulate marks of evidence, as I have done in this chapter. And to a certain extent he may evaluate these marks, by noting how much or how little knowledge they would allow. I believe I am justified in saying, with respect to the criterion—the set of marks—I have proposed, that it avoids some of the defects of empiricism and some of the excesses of the unqualified "taking" criterion. I

---

[30] There are, of course, many difficult philosophical questions about remembering that I haven't touched upon here; compare E. J. Furlong, *A Study in Memory* (London, 1951) and R. F. Holland, "The Empiricist Theory of Memory," *Mind*, LXIII (1954), pp. 464–486.

have noted, however, that we cannot evaluate a criterion with any significant degree of exactness unless we make use of the logic of confirmation.

Can we say, given our present criteria, that the propositions of electronics or of quantum physics are evident? More exactly: can we say, of those people commonly believed to be experts in these fields, that they have adequate evidence for those hypotheses about electronics or quantum mechanics which they claim to know? These technical questions are hardly within my competence. And no one can answer them without applying the logic of confirmation, or probability, to the "total evidence" at any time of the experts in question—to all of those propositions which, at that time, those experts "sensibly take" to be true, or think they remember having sensibly taken to be true, and to all of those propositions describing their "takings" and other believings at that time—and then ascertaining whether the hypotheses about electronics or quantum mechanics which they claim to know at that time are more probable than not in relation to that total evidence.

Without undertaking such difficult tasks, we may yet consider one interesting philosophical question which the thought of such tasks suggests. If we were to find, after applying the logic of confirmation in the manner described, that no one, according to our theory of evidence, has adequate evidence for the hypotheses of electronics and quantum mechanics, what course should we take? Should we say that these hypotheses are *not* evident, or should we look for new marks of evidence? [31]

---

[31] Or should we revise the logic of confirmation? In what follows, I shall not consider this possibility. For I believe that, if we were in the predicament described, and if we decided to adjust the logic of confirmation to our theory of evidence and to what we want to say is known about electronics and quantum mechanics, we would find that the results of such adjustment would imply *other* statements about knowledge and evidence we would want to reject.

Seven

Knowing about Evidence

Nor could anything be more fatal to morality than that we should wish to derive it from examples. For every example of it that is set before me must be first itself tested by principles of morality, whether it is worthy to serve as an original example.—Kant, *Fundamental Principles of the Metaphysic of Morals*

To judge of the apparances that we receive of subjects, we had need have a judicatorie instrument: to verifie this instrument, we should have demonstration; and to approve demonstration, an instrument: thus are we ever turning round.—Montaigne, *Essayes*

1. If we know that charity is a mark of what is right, then any test enabling us to decide that a certain act is an instance of charity would also enable us to decide that the act is right. If we *know* that the act is a charitable one, we also know that it is right. Hence, to the general question "How do you tell whether or not a given act is right?" we may be tempted to reply: "By finding out whether or not it has a 'right-making'

characteristic." But to the question "How do you tell whether or not a given characteristic is a 'right-making' characteristic?" we must reply, as we saw in Chapter Three: "By finding out whether or not it applies to actions which are right."

How, then, did we come to decide that acts of charity are right? More generally, how do we learn *which* characteristics are the ones that are "right-making"?

The relation of *evidence* to what I have called the "marks of evidence" is like that of *right* to what philosophers have called the "right-making" characteristics. Concerning both relations, we may ask the same sort of puzzling—and difficult —questions.

2.   Should we say that ostensible ethical generalizations, such as "Every act of charity is right," are *analytic* statements and thus, in one important sense, not really generalizations at all? If "Every act of charity is right" is analytic, then it is like "Every square is rectangular" and "Every quadruped has feet" in that its denial is contradictory and in that the meaning of the predicate term may be said to be included in that of the subject. But we have said that a "right-making" characteristic, such as we are supposing charity to be, is one we can describe in language which is "ethically neutral." *Being charitable* can be described without using "right" or any term synonymous with "right." And, more generally, it is one thing to say, of some "right-making" characteristic, that it applies to a certain action and it is quite another thing to say that that action is *right*. A man who is morally perverse may affirm that a certain act is an act of charity and yet deny that it is right. We may condemn his moral judgment; but we would not condemn his *logic*, as we would if he were to deny that some squares are rectangles. It would seem to be a mistake, then, to identify the characteristic of *being right* with any of those characteris-

tics which go to make up being charitable.[1] And therefore it would also seem to be a mistake to say, of the statement "Every act of charity is right," that it is an analytic statement.

But if "Every act of charity is right" is a *synthetic* statement, it is quite unlike the ordinary generalizations of science. Although we have spoken of "marks of rightness," the relation of *being a "right-making" characteristic*—in our example, *being an act of charity*—to *being right* is not like that of symptom to disorder. If doctors know that there is some symptom—say, a certain marking on the skin—which is invariably accompanied by neuritis, their information was acquired, presumably, as a result of someone's inductions. People who display the symptoms were examined, people who display neuritis were examined, and it was noticed that all of the people in the first class were also members of the second. But it would not be accurate to say that "Every act of charity is right" was ever established or confirmed in the same sort of way. It would not be accurate to say that someone examined certain people who were found to be acting charitably, then examined certain people who were found to be acting rightly, and then noticed that all of the people in the first group were also in the second. Professor Ayer has put this point by saying that ethical generalizations, about the goodness or badness of certain types of situation, or the rightness or wrongness of certain types of action, are not "scientific" generalizations. For if they *were* scientific generalizations, he writes,

---

[1] Bentham, according to Sidgwick, having seen that "being conducive to the general happiness" is a sign or mark of rightness, made the mistake of supposing that rightness is the *same* as being conducive to the general happiness (Henry Sidgwick, *Methods of Ethics* [London, 1893], p. 26). Bentham's mistake, if Sidgwick's charge is justified, was that of supposing that being "right-making" is the same as being right. This mistake is one form of what G. E. Moore has called the "naturalistic fallacy." We will encounter another form of the fallacy in Chapter Nine, Section 5.

then the goodness or badness of the situation, the rightness or wrongness of the action, would have to be something apart from the situation, something independently verifiable, for which the facts adduced as reasons for the moral judgment were evidence. But in these moral cases the two coincide. There is no procedure of examining the value of the facts, as distinct from examining the facts themselves. We may say that we have evidence for our moral judgments, but we cannot distinguish between pointing to the evidence itself and pointing to that for which it is supposed to be evidence. Which means that in the scientific sense it is not evidence at all.[2]

If we believe that charity is an invariable mark of rightness, we do not even feel the need to justify our belief by means of an inductive generalization; we do not feel the need to take samples or perform experiments. Why take the trouble to examine acts of charity to *find out* whether they are right? An "experiment in the imagination" will do. We need only *think about* various types of charitable action and if we consider all the relevant possibilities we will then be in a position to decide whether or not every act of charity is right.

But if someone were to *disagree* with us, holding that charity is *not* a "right-making" characteristic, or even holding that charity is "wrong-making," that every act of charity would be *wrong*, what kind of argument or evidence could we use to show him that he was mistaken? We cannot establish our own

---

[2] A. J. Ayer, *Philosophical Essays* (London, 1954), p. 237. Compare the following quotation from *Butler's Moral Philosophy*, by Austin Duncan-Jones: "If there are categorical obligations, and if no statement that a categorical obligation exists can be resolved into statements about obligation-bearing qualities; and if, further, no amount of knowledge about obligation-bearing qualities would, by itself, tell us what our obligations were, it follows that knowledge of obligation—supposing that we can know them—must be obtained by some quite distinct process, different from any process by which we get to know the facts of the physical world, or human history, or human psychology" (p. 162).

moral principle—that every act of charity would be *right*—by the usual inductive procedure of science, nor can we establish it by showing it to be a consequence of the principles of logic or mathematics.[3]

3. All of the foregoing applies, *mutatis mutandis*, to the relation between *evidence* and *marks of evidence*, to the relation between evidence and "evidence-bearing" characteristics. The statement that being appeared to, or that taking, is a mark of evidence is not an analytic statement; it is not like "All squares are rectangles." Nor is it a statement which seems to require— or which could have—any inductive evidence.[4] If we are able to make a decision about such a statement, if we can decide whether or not to accept it, then we can do so merely by thinking of the various possibilities and without "examining" particular cases. For epistemic reasoning and discourse are very much like ethical reasoning and discourse.

In opposing Clifford's ethics of belief, I suggested, in Chapter One, that a proposition should be regarded as innocent until proven guilty, that we may accept any proposition we would like to accept provided only that we do not have adequate evidence for its contradictory. In saying this, I was guided, in part, by what I believed to be the skeptical consequences of accepting Clifford's ethics. If Clifford were to reject my

---

[3] See Bertrand Russell's account of a debate between Buddha and Nietzsche, in his *A History of Western Philosophy* (New York, 1945), pp. 770 ff. Compare C. L. Stevenson, "The Nature of Ethical Disagreement," in H. Feigl and W. S. Sellars, eds., *Readings in Philosophical Analysis* (New York, 1949).

[4] We must distinguish between (i) confirming that something is a mark of evidence and (ii) confirming that some mark of evidence is a mark of truth. We saw in Chapter Three, Section 3, that, given certain marks of evidence, (ii) is possible; the above paragraph, however, pertains to (i).

reasoning, if he were to say that no demonstration of skeptical consequences would invalidate his principle, our dispute would be like an ethical one and we would have difficulty in settling upon any method of resolving it.

Presenting "the problem of the criterion" in Chapter Three, I suggested that we cannot decide what any of the marks of evidence are—we cannot decide what characteristics or events are "evidence-making"—until we are able to say which of our beliefs are evident. If we are able to show that we have a rule, enabling us to distinguish good apples from bad apples, then we know which apples are bad and which apples are good. And if we are to choose among a number of such rules, our decision will depend, in part, upon what we know about the goodness and badness of the apples.

In the previous chapter, we chose among a number of possible marks of evidence and we made our decision, apparently, by reference to what we knew about the kind of evidence that is available to us. We rejected "empiricism" because of what we judged to be its defects: for empiricism seems to imply, as Hume had seen, that it is in vain for us to ask whether there be body. We rejected the unqualified "taking" criterion because of what we judged to be its excesses: for, if we accept the "taking" criterion, then we must say, of what seem to be the most unacceptable of prejudices, that they are constantly made evident in the experience of those who have them. And we said, of the "sensibly-taking" criterion, that it seemed to be acceptable: for if we accept the "sensibly-taking" criterion, then, apparently, we can describe as evident just those propositions which we *want* to describe as evident. And therefore we may say, in reply to the question with which we concluded the previous chapter: "If, according to the 'sensibly-taking' criterion, no one has adequate evidence for the propositions of

electronics and quantum physics, and if we *want* to be able
to say that these propositions are evident to someone, then we
may reject the 'sensibly-taking' criterion."

In his *History of Western Philosophy*, Bertrand Russell said
that St. Thomas has "little of the true philosophic spirit." For
St. Thomas, according to Russell, "is not engaged in an inquiry, the result of which it is impossible to know in advance.
Before he begins to philosophize, he already knows the truth;
it is declared in the Catholic Faith." [5] But similarly, when we
set out to solve the problem of the criterion, we already knew
which propositions are the ones that are evident; we knew in
advance that skepticism with regard to the senses is mistaken.
Hence one might say that, if St. Thomas' philosophy constitutes "special pleading" for certain propositions of theology,
our philosophy constitutes "special pleading" for certain propositions of science and common sense.[6]

What if a theologian or a mystic were to tell us that no
criterion of evidence is adequate unless it describes marks of
evidence enabling us to say that there are people who have
evidence for certain propositions about God and his attributes?

Leon Chwistek, describing the epistemic principles, which
most of us profess, as the "criteria of sound reason," considers
a bookkeeper who, in a moment of fatigue, loses his faith in

---

[5] Russell, A *History of Western Philosophy*, p. 463.

[6] Compare Russell's own description of the inquiry he was later to undertake in his *Human Knowledge*: "If I ever have the leisure to undertake another serious investigation of a philosophical problem, I shall attempt to
analyse the inferences from experience to the world of physics, assuming
them capable of validity, and seeking to discover what principles of inference, if true, would make them valid. Whether these principles, when
discovered, are accepted as true, is a matter of temperament; what should
not be a matter of temperament should be the proof that acceptance of
them is necessary if solipsism is to be rejected" (quoted from "My Mental
Development," in P. A. Schilpp, ed., *The Philosophy of Bertrand Russell*
[The Library of Living Philosophers, vol. V, Evanston, Ill., 1944], p. 16).

these criteria. If the bookkeeper's friends cannot lead him out of this situation, they will

regard him as insane and put him in a sanitarium. In such an event he obviously will not believe that he has been justly treated. On the contrary, he will be convinced that the concept of reality [evidence] they employ in putting him out of the way is not worthy of serious consideration. To the argument that it is not possible to remain alive for long if daily life is disregarded, he could simply retort: Why should one remain alive? It is far better really to have enjoyed one brief glimpse of true reality than to have lived in unenlightened error for a long time.[7]

Can we say, to the skeptic, the mystic, and the bookkeeper, that the procedure we have followed is not itself an instance of "special pleading"? Can we say, concerning the propositions *we* want to count as evident, that they are propositions which, prior to our philosophical inquiry, we *knew* to be evident? Can we say, more generally, that *epistemic* statements express propositions for which we can have evidence, or which we can know to be true? [8]

---

[7] Leon Chwistek, *The Limits of Science* (New York, 1948), pp. 288–289. Chwistek adds that "although there is no way of convincing the over-tired bookkeeper that the multiplication table is correct, there are no good reasons to question it."

[8] This "objective" conception has been clearly and explicitly defended in scholastic writings on epistemology; among the best of these, I think, are Cardinal Mercier's *Critériologie générale* and P. Coffey's *Epistemology* (London, 1917). In *Human Knowledge*, Russell makes use of the undefined term "degree of credibility" and says this about our knowledge of credibility: "We must hold that the degree of credibility attached to a proposition is itself sometimes a datum. I think we should also hold that the degree of credibility to be attached to a *datum* is sometimes a datum, and sometimes (perhaps always) falls short of certainty. We may hold, in such a case, that there is only one datum, namely a proposition with a degree of credibility attached to it, or we may hold that the datum and its degree of credibility are two separate data. I shall not consider which of these two views should be adopted" (pp. 381–382). Compare G. E. Moore, *Some*

Perceiving

Much of what may be said of our knowledge of *ethics*, or right and wrong, may also be said about our knowledge of *evidence*. In what follows, let us consider our ethical and epistemic convictions together. I use the word "conviction" instead of "belief," and instead of "approval" and "disapproval," in order not to prejudge the issues that will be raised.

4. It is illuminating to compare our ethical and epistemic convictions with our *feelings* or *emotions*. For many of the statements in which we express our feelings and emotions resemble the ethical and epistemic statements we have been discussing.

If we were to approach "the theory of humor" in the way we have approached the theories of ethics and evidence, we would try to formulate general propositions relating the ostensible characteristic of *being amusing* to the *marks* of being amusing— to "amusement-bearing" qualities. Combining various suggestions which have been made about humor, a philosopher might say: "Whenever a pretentious person is exhibited as functioning like a machine, then, provided the exhibition is surprising but not completely implausible, it is amusing." The philosopher's statement could be construed in the way we have construed the ethical and epistemic statements of our examples. We could show that his statement is not analytic; a man could deny the statement without contradicting himself. And we could show that his statement is not a synthetic statement arrived at by inductive procedures. It is not a statement which can be falsified by showing, say, that, Navahos are *not* amused

Problems of Philosophy (London, 1953), chs. vi and vii; H. A. Prichard, "Does Moral Philosophy Rest upon a Mistake?" *Mind*, vol. XXI (1912), reprinted in Prichard's *Moral Obligation* and in W. S. Sellars and John Hospers, eds., *Readings in Ethical Theory* (New York, 1952); and C. I. Lewis, *An Analysis of Knowledge and Valuation*, ch. xi.

in the situations described. For (our philosopher could say) if Navahos do not laugh under the condition he has described, then either their sense of humor is perverted or it is not yet developed.[9] To decide whether or not to accept the general statement about *being amusing*, we do not need to examine actual cases. It is enough to "examine possible cases"—to think about various possible situations and then to decide, with respect to each, whether or not it *would* be amusing. And therefore, our philosopher might conclude, his generalization is a *synthetic* statement we can know *a priori* to be true.

But it is simpler to say that *being amused* is not a state which is either true or false. Being amused at the comedian's dance is *not* like expecting the post office soon to be painted. If I expect the post office to be painted, then I am in a state which is true if and only if the post office *is* about to be painted. And the words in which I express this state—"The post office is soon to be painted"—are, similarly, true if and only if the post office *is* soon to be painted. But if I am amused at the comedian's dance, my amusement is not thereby true or false. I may express my amusement in the indicative sentence "The comedian's dance is funny." But we need not say, of my state and of the words which express it, that "they are true if and only if the comedian's dance *is* funny."

To say that the dance is funny is to report or express the fact that one is amused; it is *not* to say that the dance has a certain characteristic in virtue of which one's laughter or amusement is *correct* or *true*. But to say that the post office will soon be painted is to say more than that one believes or expects that

---

[9] In *The Philosophy of B*rt*nd R*ss*ll*, Philip E. B. Jourdain speaks of "the surprising method" of those moral philosophers "who expect to discover what *is* good by inquiring what cannibals have *thought* good" (p. 86). In Chapter Nine, Section 5, I shall discuss the relation of such generalizations to ethical statements. Cf. A. I. Melden, in Richard Brandt, ed., *Science, Language, and Human Rights* (Philadelphia, 1952), esp. pp. 174–175.

the post office will soon be painted; it is to say, rather, that the post office has a certain characteristic—or is going to have a certain characteristic—in virtue of which one's belief, or expectation, is true. I think that most people would say, more generally, with respect to our feelings or emotions, that even though these feelings or emotions may frequently be said to have objects—one may be pleased, or disturbed, or unconcerned, about some *x* being *f*—these feelings are neither true nor false, neither correct nor mistaken.[10]

Since the statements expressing what I have called our ethical and epistemic convictions resemble some of those expressing our emotions or feelings, and since the respect in which they resemble the statements expressing our emotions or feelings is one in which they differ from the generalizations of science and mathematics, we may be tempted to say that our ethical and epistemic convictions *also* resemble our emotions or feelings in being neither true nor false, in being neither correct nor mistaken. If we decide to say this, then the terms "approval" and "disapproval" may be more accurate in the present context than the word "conviction." The statement "He morally approved of the official's refusal to testify" would be like "He was amused by the comedian's dance," and unlike "He expected the post office soon to be painted," in that the verb is *not* replaceable by "believe" and an adjective designating some characteristic. "He morally approved of the official's re-

---

[10] For our present purposes, we may count *desire* as a type of "feeling" or "emotion." Saying that a man desires something *correctly* must be distinguished, of course, from saying that his desire is *not in vain*, and saying that he desires something *mistakenly* must be distinguished from saying that his desire is *in vain*. A man's desire to visit France may be said to be "not in vain" if and only if he does visit France. But his desire would be *correct* if and only if his visiting France had a certain characteristic—presumably that of being *desirable*—in *virtue* of which the desire would *be* correct: hence a desire which is in vain might be correct and one which is mistaken might be not in vain.

fusal to testify" would *not* mean that the official's refusal to testify had a certain characteristic—that of *being right*—in virtue of which the moral approval was either true or false.

Some of the philosophers who have taken this view of our ethical or epistemic convictions—or, rather, of our ethical or epistemic *approvals* and *disapprovals*—have said that the statements in which we ostensibly express these approvals and disapprovals have the same meaning as do the statements in which we might *report* these approvals and disapprovals. If a man says, "The official acted rightly in refusing to betray his friends," then, according to this "psychologistic" conception, he is saying merely, "I approve of the official's refusal to betray his friends." And if a man says, "It would be unreasonable to suppose that the crisis will soon be over," then, according to this conception, he is saying merely, "I disapprove of accepting the hypothesis that the crisis will soon be over." Hence, if we accept this conception, we could say that, even if our approvals and disapprovals are neither true nor false, neither correct nor mistaken, our ethical and epistemic *statements* are statements which are either true or false. Similarly, even though the state of being amused is neither true nor false, neither correct nor mistaken, such statements as "That dance was very funny" are either true or false. For "That dance was very funny" is a *report* of someone's amusement: "I was very amused by that dance."

This "psychologistic" interpretation of our ethical and epistemic convictions has at least one implausible consequence. If "psychologism" were true, then, in order to show that a particular moral or epistemic statement is true, it would be sufficient to show that the person who made the statement did in fact make the appraisal which such a statement would normally express. And in order to show that such a statement is false, it would be sufficient to show that the person did *not*

Perceiving

make the appraisal which the statement would normally express. For example, in order to show that "The official's act was right" is true, it would be sufficient to show that the person who made the statement approved of the official's act; and in order to show that it is false, it would be sufficient to show that the person did not approve of the official's act.[11]

If we are to say that our moral and epistemic convictions—our approvals and disapprovals—are *neither* true nor false, it would seem reasonable also to say that the statements in which these approvals and disapprovals are normally expressed are, similarly, neither true nor false. Instead of interpreting these statements "psychologistically," we might interpret them "emotively," or "performatively." We could say that such statements as "He acted rightly" and "That hypothesis is unreasonable" are like "Would that he were to return," "The Lord be praised," and "Do not cross the street," which are *not* used to say what could be true or false. These statements perform a variety of linguistic functions: they express or give vent to one's feelings; they influence the behavior and feelings of other people; and they are used to make ceremony. But according to this "emotive" conception, they are not used to say what is true or false. And the approvals and disapprovals which they express are not states which are true or false.[12]

---

[11] Compare the criticism of "psychologism" in Gottlob Frege, *Die Grundlagen der Arithmetiq* (Breslau, 1884), pp. 36–38; Edmund Husserl, *Logische Untersuchungen* (Halle, 1929), I, 50–191; Désiré Mercier, *Critériologie générale*, pp. 172–217; A. Meinong, "Für die Psychologie und gegen den Psychologismus in der allgemeinen Werttheorie," *Logos*, III (1912), 1–14; and Rudolf Carnap, *Logical Foundations of Probability*, pp. 37–42.

[12] Anders Wedberg, in "Bertrand Russell's Empiricism," has suggested that our inability to use the terms "knowledge" and "true belief" interchangeably "is explained by the fact that 'knowledge' expresses something which the phrase 'true belief' does not express, namely an actual belief feeling of a special kind" (*Adolf Phalén in Memoriam* [Uppsala, 1937], p. 351). See also C. H. Whiteley, "More about Probability," *Analysis*, vol. VIII (1948); R. F. Atkinson, " 'Good,' 'Right,' and 'Probable,' in *Language*,

Knowing about Evidence

We could accept an "emotive," or "performative," interpretation of *epistemic* statements and yet retain an "objective" interpretation of *probability* statements. For it is convenient to restrict "probability" to those statements which describe relative frequencies or which state the degree of confirmation that one hypothesis may have in relation to another. As we saw in Chapter Two, however, such probability statements will not tell us anything of epistemic significance—will not tell us what is evident or what we have a right to believe—unless we apply the principles of probability to statements for which we have adequate evidence.[13]

The "emotive," or "performative," conception of ethical and epistemic statements shares the economy and simplicity of "psychologism" without having its implausible consequences. We need no longer say that, in order to show that "The official acted rightly" is true, it is sufficient to show that the person who said it did in fact approve of the official's action. For we can no longer say that "The official acted rightly" is true.

But what reason do we have for saying that our ethical and epistemic convictions—our approvals and disapprovals—are neither true nor false? If we can find a good reason for accepting such a view of ethical statements and convictions, we can also find a good reason for accepting such a view of epistemic statements and convictions.

5. Those who say that our ethical convictions are neither true nor false often appeal to arguments which are inconclusive.

Truth, and Logic," *Mind*, vol. LXIV; and Stephen Toulmin, "Probability," *Proceedings of the Aristotelian Society*, Suppl. vol. XXIV (1950).

[13] J. N. Findlay suggests an "emotive" interpretation of probability statements in "Probability without Nonsense," *Philosophical Quarterly*, II (1952), 218–219. But he does not restrict "probability" in the way I have proposed; I believe we may say that his discussion applies only to those probability statements which meet the two epistemic conditions I described in Chapter Two.

They may point out (i) that no statement is true or false unless it is a "factual" or "descriptive" statement and (ii) that the statements which express our moral convictions are not "factual" or "descriptive." (The technical terms I have put in quotation marks may, of course, be replaced by others—for instance, by "scientific," "verifiable," or "cognitive.") But we find, on analyzing such arguments, that one of the two premises (it may be either) is taken to be analytic—as derivable from statements explicating the terms in quotation marks—and that the other premise is not defended at all.[14]

The best reason for saying that our moral and epistemic convictions are neither true nor false seems to me to be this: If we say, of these convictions and of the statements in which they are expressed, that they *are* either true or false, and if we say, further, that some of them can be *known* to be true or to be false, then, as I have noted, we seem committed to saying that there are synthetic statements, about ethics and about evidence, which we know *a priori* to be true or to be false. Hence, to avoid the doctrine of the synthetic *a priori*, we may classify moral and epistemic convictions with such states as that of *being amused* and say that they are *neither* true nor false. The view that such convictions and the statements expressing them are neither true nor false is simpler and more economical than its contradictory and leads to fewer puzzling questions.

We should remind ourselves, however, that "simplicity" and "economy" alone do *not* constitute sufficient reason for accepting any view, philosophical or otherwise. One might argue that our ostensible beliefs about the past are really not beliefs —that they are attitudes which are neither true nor false—and that the statements in which they are expressed ("I saw him

---

[14] If *both* premises are taken to be analytic, our problem becomes that of deciding whether what we have here been calling "moral convictions" *are* moral convictions.

Knowing about Evidence

at the meeting yesterday"), although capable of performing many linguistic functions, are neither true nor false. Such a conception would have the advantage of economy and simplicity, for it would dispense with the notion of the past and thus enable us to avoid a number of puzzling questions about our memory. A similar conception might be applied to the notion of *future*, or to that of *time* generally. In these instances, however, the economy and simplicity of the view in question do not constitute a sufficient reason for accepting it.[15]

Yet there is one significant difference between our beliefs about the past and our moral and epistemic convictions. In discussing the concept of *sensibly taking*, in the previous chapter, we described a source of evidence—other than seeming-to-remember—for statements about the past. We said that if, with respect to two events, a man *takes* one of them to occur before the other, he thereby has adequate evidence for believing that the one occurred before the other. We said the words "before" and "after" describe certain sensible relations. There is a respect, therefore, in which the concept of something being *past* can be said to be exemplified in our experience.[16] But there

---

[15] Compare C. I. Lewis, *An Analysis of Knowledge and Valuation*, p. 320; "For one who should lack a primordial sense of probable events [of evidence], every attempted explanation of a categorical probability statement must fail. And who should perversely insist upon reduction of its meaning to terms of some presently ascertained factuality—other than the data given rise to it —must simply be left behind in the discussion. He denies a category of cognition which is fundamental and as different from theoretically certain knowledge as apprehension of the future is different from observation of the present."

[16] Compare E. J. Furlong, *A Study in Memory* (London, 1951), p. 104: "We do not see the pastness of a remembered event in the same immediate way as we see the greenness of a green surface. We do, however, find instances of pastness elsewhere, namely in the specious present. From these instances we learn to think of a past that stretches beyond the limits of the specious present, even beyond the beginnings of our own experience, beyond the advent of life on the earth."

111

is no similar respect in which the concepts of *rightness* or of *evidence* can be said to be exemplified in our experience. For we did not say that the word "evidence"—or "good" or "right" —describes any sensible characteristic. Our theory of evidence, it could be said, does not allow anyone to have evidence for statements about evidence; it doesn't tell us that there is anything which is a *mark of evidence* for statements about evidence.

In formulating our theory of evidence, we seem to have been guided by what, in advance, we wished to regard as evident. The good apples had already been separated from the bad ones. What, then, if the mystic or the bookkeeper had expressed a different conception? Suppose the mystic or the bookkeeper had classified the apples differently—and, in consequence, had described some other experiences as marks of evidence?

I do not feel that we can reply to the mystic and the bookkeeper unless we are prepared to accept the doctrine of the synthetic *a priori*.

PART III

The Objects of Perception

Eight

Sensing

1. There is no contradiction in saying, "I realize there aren't any centaurs, but that strange animal certainly does *look* centaurian." For the statement "That animal looks centaurian" does not imply that there *is* anything centaurian; it does not imply that there are any centaurs. "The pail feels empty" and "The woods sound inhabited" do not imply that there is an appearance which is empty or one which is inhabited; "The curtains appear green" does not imply that there is an appearance—or a way of appearing—which is green. And, more generally, the locution

(1) x appears . . . to S

does not imply

There is something which is . . . .

Should we say that "centaurian" in "That animal looks centaurian" attributes some *other* property to the look of the animal—some property other than that of being a centaur? And should we say of "green" in "The curtains appear green" that it attributes some *other* property to the appearance of the curtains—some property other than that of being green? What would these properties be? If we are not saying of the look of the animal that it is a *centaur,* what are we saying of the look of the animal? And if we are not saying of the appearance of the curtains that it is *green,* what are we saying of the appearance of the curtains? The answer, obviously, is that "The animal looks centaurian" doesn't attribute anything to the "look of the animal" and "The curtains appear green" doesn't attribute anything to the appearance of the curtains.

The adjectives or adverbs qualifying the verb in locutions such as (1) must not be taken as predicating some characteristic of the thing the verb refers to. Rather, the complex expressions consisting of the verb followed by its modifier—the expressions "looks centaurian" and "appear green"—attribute something to what the noun, or subject of the verb, refers to. These complex expressions, whether we take them comparatively or noncomparatively, might thus be replaced by single words—for example, by "lookscentaurian" and "appearsgreen."

It is true that "look," "sound," and other appear words are sometimes used without adjectives or other ostensibly qualifying expressions. We may say, for example, "I like the way it sounds" or "Tell me how it looks." When appear words are used in this way, they may be thought of as designating genera, of which "looks green" and "sounds loud" designate more determinate species. The relation of "looks green" to "looks" is that of "green" to "color," not that of "green" to "apple."

We should be on our guard, therefore, when locution (1) above is transformed as

(2) x presents a . . . appearance to S.

For statements of the form of (2) are deceptively like such

statements as "John presents an expensive gift to Mary," where the adjective attributes a property to the thing designated by the noun following it. The locutions "*x* takes on a . . . appearance for S," "S senses a . . . appearance of *x*," and "S is acquainted with a . . . sense-datum belonging to *x*," which may be thought of as variants of (2), are equally misleading. Whatever else appearances may be, then, they are not "objects to a subject." [1]

2.   But Bishop Berkeley said that, if an oar with one end in the water looks crooked, then what one "immediately perceives by sight *is* certainly crooked." [2] And other philosophers seem also to have thought that appearances are objects to a subject —that our locution "*x* appears . . . to S" does entail "There is something which is . . . ." [3] And this assumption, as we should expect, often leads to difficulties.

Kant believed that, by means of the "first antinomy of pure reason," he had demonstrated the proposition (a) that nothing whatever exists in time—that no two things are such that one precedes or comes before the other. The proposition that things are in time, he thought, entails a contradiction; it entails that, for anything existing in time, the series of things preceding it *has* a beginning in time and also has *no* beginning

---

[1] G. F. Stout, "Are Presentations Mental or Physical?" *Proceedings of the Aristotelian Society*, n.s. IX (1909), 243. Compare Samuel Alexander, *Space, Time, and Deity* (London, 1920), I, 12; C. J. Ducasse, *Nature, Mind, and Death* (LaSalle, Ill., 1951), pp. 287–290; and Gilbert Ryle, *The Concept of Mind*, p. 209. This general view of appearing is also to be found in Thomas Reid's *Essays on the Intellectual Powers of Man*; see Essay I, ch. i, sec. 12.

[2] *The works of George Berkeley*, A. C. Fraser ed. (Oxford, 1901), I, 456; my italics. The quotation appears in the *Three Dialogues between Hylas and Philonous*, Third Dialogue.

[3] I should note that I made this assumption in "The Theory of Appearing," in Max Black, ed., *Philosophical Analysis*.

in time. He conceded, however, (b) that there are things which *appear* to exist in time—that some things appear to precede or come before others. And he took (b) to imply (c) that *appearances* of things do exist in time. Time, together with space, he said, constitutes the "form of intuition"—the way in which we *must* sense appearances: this form, according to Kant, "is not to be looked for in the object in itself but in the subject to which the object appears; nevertheless it belongs really and necessarily to the appearance of this object." [4] Kant did not notice, apparently, that his propositions (a) and (c) are contradictory. For if appearances really and necessarily are in time, then it is false to say that nothing whatever exists in time. [5]

It was a similar mistake, I think, which once led Professor Ayer to suggest that the appearance of a striped tiger could have many stripes and yet no definite number of stripes. The stripes on a tiger, he said, may "look to be numerous" and yet they may not "look to be of any definite number." And therefore, he inferred, we may say of the appearance of the tiger "that it contains a number of stripes without containing any definite number." [6]

There are philosophers who would say, similarly, that if a black piece of coal happens to look blue, then there is a certain thing *a*—not the piece of coal but its appearance or way of looking—which *is* blue. The appearance or way of looking, *a*, has at least one attribute which it shares with many physical things; for *a*, like the cars on the Arlberg Express, is blue. And such philosophers would say, presumably, that one finds *a* to have this attribute by looking at the piece of coal. But now we

[4] *The Critique of Pure Reason*, B 55; Norman Kemp Smith ed., p. 80.

[5] Compare the criticism of Kant in H. A. Prichard, *Kant's Theory of Knowledge* (Oxford, 1909), ch. iv, and G. E. Moore, *Some Problems of Philosophy*, p. 170.

[6] A. J. Ayer, *Philosophical Essays*, p. 93.

may ask the puzzling philosophical question: "Does *a* have any *other* attributes which are also attributes of some physical things, but which one cannot learn about in this way—which one cannot learn about by looking at the piece of coal and finding out how *it* appears?"

Some of the philosophers who have faced such questions have then gone on to ask: Do appearances, like the things that present them, have surfaces, as well as parts which are behind or beneath these surfaces, and rear surfaces which face away? [7] G. E. Moore once suggested—though with some hesitation— that appearances, or "sense-data," may possibly *appear* to have certain attributes which they do not have in fact:

that the sense-datum which corresponds to a penny, which I am seeing obliquely, is not really perceived to *be* different in shape from that which corresponded to the penny, when I was straight in front of it, but is only perceived to *seem* different—that all that is perceived is that the one *seems* elliptical and the other circular.[8]

It is important to realize that we cannot avoid such puzzling questions merely by redefining the word "appearance." We could define "appearance" in such a way that we could say of any appearance, as Professor Price has said, that its goods "are entirely in the shop-window." [9] We could define "the appearance of a piece of coal" as being something which has just those attributes which the coal appears to have.[10] And then, of

---

[7] See H. H. Price, *Perception*, pp. 105–109, 131; Konrad Marc-Wogau, *Die Theorie der Sinnesdaten* (Uppsala, 1945), chs. iv, v, and vi; C. D. Broad, "Professor Marc-Wogau's *Theorie der Sinnesdaten* (II), *Mind*, LVI (1947), especially 108–109; and C. A. Baylis, "The Given and Perceptual Knowledge," in Marvin Farber, ed., *Philosophic Thought in France and the United States* (Buffalo, 1950).

[8] G. E. Moore, *Philosophical Studies* (London, 1922), p. 245.

[9] Price, *Perception*, p. 145.

[10] Compare the definition in A. J. Ayer, *Foundations of Empirical Knowledge*, p. 58.

course, we could be sure that the appearance of the coal doesn't have a rear surface or any parts which face away. But now we may ask of *a*—the something which is blue when the coal looks blue—whether *a is* an appearance, as just defined, of the piece of coal. And this question can be answered only by deciding whether *a* has a rear surface or any parts which "face away."

But if what I have said is true, we do not meet with such questions. For "*x* appears so-and-so" does not imply that there is anything which is so-and-so.[11]

3. We have contrasted the "appearing" terminology of

(1) *x* appears . . . to S

with the "appearance" terminology of

(2) *x* presents a . . . appearance to S.

And we have noted that (2) is convertible in the following way:

(3) S senses a . . . appearance of *x*.

Comparing these three locutions, we now see that there is another possibility, one which is related to (3) in the way in which (1) is related to (2):

(4) S senses . . . with respect to *x*.

The term "senses" we here introduce may be taken as synonymous with the awkward expression "is appeared to" used in

---

[11] George Paul has noted still other problems which arise when we assume that there are appearances ("sense-data") having some of the characteristics of physical things: "Is There a Problem about Sense-Data?" *Proceedings of the Aristotelian Society,* suppl. vol. XV, reprinted in Antony Flew, ed., *Logic and Language,* 1st ser. Compare A. E. Murphy, *The Uses of Reason* (New York, 1943), pp. 32–45. In the following chapter, I shall consider one possible reason for saying that there are "appearances" having some of the characteristics of some physical things.

Part II; or, better, (4) may be taken as synonymous with "S is appeared to . . . by x."

We may obtain variants of these forms by using a different terminology. For example, the verb and preposition in (2) may be replaced, respectively, by "take on" and "for." In place of "senses" in (3), we may substitute a different verb, say "experiences," "intuits," "is aware of," or even "has"; and in place of "appearance," we may substitute a different noun, say, "sensum" or "sense-datum." Some philosophers, using locution (3) have replaced the preposition "of" by the phrase "which belongs to." But, unless we question the mode of designating the perceiver and the object, we are not likely to want to describe the experiences in any other type of locution.

It is true that the expression "perceive as" is sometimes used in such contexts. Instead of saying (1) that x appears red to S or (2) that x presents a red appearance to S, we could say that x is *perceived as* red by S. And instead of saying (3) that S senses a red appearance of x or (4) that S senses red with respect to x, we could say that S *perceives x as* red.[12] We could also use "see," "hear," "smell," "feel," and "taste" in this way. We could say that one sees the stick as bent, hears the music as Arabian, tastes the wine as Burgundy, and so on. But there are a number of reasons for avoiding this way of speaking. For

---

[12] In *Berkeley* (London, 1953), G. J. Warnock suggests that, instead of saying "something appears . . . to me," we say, "It seems to me as if I were perceiving (seeing, hearing, etc.) something which is . . ." (pp. 169 ff.). I avoid this type of locution, however, because I attempt to define the two most important uses of perception words in terms of "appear." Although Warnock's discussion is in general an excellent one, he does not, I believe, recognize the possibility of using appear words "noncomparatively." I would make similar comments with regard to O. K. Bouwsma, "Moore's Theory of Sense-Data," in P. A. Schilpp, ed., *The Philosophy of G. E. Moore*, and Richard Wollheim, "The Difference between Sensing and Observing," *Proceedings of the Aristotelian Society*, suppl. vol. XXVIII (1954).

one thing, "S perceives x as red" is often taken to imply "S takes x to *be* red." But our locution must not have this implication; we want to be able to say that x appears red to S without implying that S takes x to be red. And, for another thing, the "perceives as" terminology, unlike two of the terminologies listed above, happens to be inadequate for describing certain "nonperceptual" experiences. The most satisfactory terminology will be one which enables us to describe, not only appearing, but also the experiences involved in dreaming, remembering, and imagining, in being hallucinated, and in having such disturbances as "spots before the eyes" and "ringing noises in the ears."

Of a man who has "spots before his eyes," for example, we could say, following (3), that he senses "a spotty appearance." But we need not add, as we do in (3), that the appearance is *of* anything; indeed, we could add in this instance that the appearance is *not* an appearance *of* anything. Or we can say, following (4), that the man senses (is appeared to) "spottily," or "in a spotty manner." But we need not add, as we do in (4), that he senses (is appeared to) "with respect to" any object. If, however, we try to describe this experience in the terminology of *appearing,* or of *appearances,* we find new questions in our way. To fit the spots into the appearing terminology of (1), we must refer to some object x which happens to be appearing "in a spotty manner." And to fit them into the appearance terminology of (2), we must refer to some object x which "presents a spotty appearance." But what could this object x be? If a man has "spots before his eyes," it may well be that none of the things he is looking at, or none of the things that are stimulating his eyes, *appear* spotty or *present* spotty appearances. And, similarly, if a man has "a ringing in his ears," it may be that none of the things he is listening to, or none of the things that are stimulating his ears, *sound* in

Sensing

this ringing way to him or *present* him with ringing sounds.

Our talk about *pains* and other such feelings is, of course, easily adapted to the terminology of sensing. Instead of saying "I have a pain" or "I experience a pain," we may say, if we choose, "I sense painfully." By talking in this rather odd way, we are able to avoid one group of questions about "other minds" which some recent philosophers have discussed at considerable length. "Can another person experience *my* pains? Is it logically possible for the pain that one man experiences to be *identical* with the pain that another man experiences?" We cannot formulate such questions in the sensing terminology. We no longer have the noun "pain"; hence we cannot use "pain" as subject of the phrase "is identical with"; and therefore we cannot ask whether another person can experience *my* pains.

In a similar way, we avoid the puzzling questions about the relations between appearances—"visual sense-data"—and the surfaces of physical things. No longer having such expressions as "elliptical sense-datum," we cannot ask whether "the elliptical sense-datum is identical with the round penny which presents it."

If we were to restrict ourselves to a single one of the four locutions above, we would find (4)—"S senses red with respect to *x*"—to be the most convenient. It is capable of describing any experience we can describe by means of the other three. Unlike (2) and (3), it does not lead to the difficulties we have associated with the terminology of *appearances*.[13] Un-

---

[13] Philosophers have often objected to the appearance, or sense-datum, terminology on the ground that it enables us to formulate such questions as "Do there exist appearances which no perceiver senses?" and "Do objects take on appearances for things other than perceiving organisms?" But the other terminologies, I think, allow similar questions. We may ask, using the terminology of appearing, "Are things other than perceiving organisms ever appeared to?" and we may ask, using the terminology of sensing, "Do

like (1), it is adequate for describing those experiences of "ringing noises" and the like which are not *appearances* of anything. And, in application to such experiences, "sensing" may be less misleading than our earlier "is appeared to."

For the purposes of our ordinary talk about the ways in which things appear, the terminology of sensing has no special advantage. But if what we want to do is to describe perceiving in that way which is least puzzling philosophically, then this strange and artificial terminology would seem to be the least misleading. The alternative terminologies entangle us in philosophical questions we can avoid if we talk in terms of sensing. For us, the important thing is merely that we recognize this fact and not that we actually adopt the terminology of sensing.

What I have said about the comparative and noncomparative uses of the locution "x appears so-and-so to S" also holds, of course, of the locution "S senses so-and-so with respect to x." And what I have said about the role of the adjectives, or the adverbs, which are used with appear words—the adjective or adverb which would replace "so-and-so" in "x appears so-and-so to S"—also holds of the adjectives or adverbs which are used with "sense."

---

things other than perceiving organisms ever sense?" (These questions may arise even though we do not take "There is a . . . ." to be a consequence of "x appears . . . ," or of "S senses. . . .") I believe that certain speculations of Whitehead and Samuel Alexander are affirmative answers to the latter two questions, in the terminologies of appearing and of sensing. I have in mind Whitehead's doctrine of "prehensions," according to which "all actual things are subjects, each prehending the universe from which it arises," and Alexander's view that we may "ascribe 'mind' to all things alike, in various degrees." See A. N. Whitehead, *Process and Reality* (Cambridge, 1930), p. 89, and Samuel Alexander, "The Basis of Realism," *Proceedings of the British Academy*, VI (1914), 32. Whitehead finds such doctrines suggested by Leibniz's theory of monads, as well as by Locke's *Essay*, bk. IV, ch. iii, sec. 6.

Given the sensing terminology, then, we may define *appear:*
"*x appears* . . . to S" means that S senses . . . with respect
to *x.*

But I have not yet said what it is to sense in a certain way
with respect to an object, what it is for an appearance to be
an appearance *of* an object. In the chapter following the next
one, I shall attempt to define this use of "with respect to"—
this use of "of"—in purely causal terms. Before attempting
this definition, however, we must first consider those powers
or dispositions that Locke described as "secondary qualities."

Nine

Secondary Qualities

1. The *secondary qualities* of physical objects, Locke said, are "such qualities, which in truth are nothing in the objects themselves, but powers to produce various sensations in us by their primary qualities, i.e., by the bulk, figure, texture and motion of their insensible parts, as colors, sounds, tastes, etc." [1] Where Locke speaks of *primary qualities* of an object, it may now be better to speak of the physical or microscopic structure of the object. But otherwise, I think, his definition remains useful.

When we investigate the secondary qualities of objects, we learn to complete statements of this sort:

If anything has . . . physical structure, then: if under . . . conditions it sensibly stimulates a perceiver who is . . . , the perceiver will sense in a . . . manner.

---

[1] John Locke, *Essay concerning Human Understanding*, bk. II, ch. viii, sec. 10. The term "secondary quality" could be construed sufficiently broadly to be coextensive with what, in Chapter Six, I referred to as "sensible qualities"; in the context of the present chapter I think Locke's term is more appropriate.

Such a statement describes the conditions under which a physical object, serving as a source of stimulation, may cause a perceiver to sense. If the principal antecedent were to describe the microscopic structure of the things I am now looking at and if the subordinate antecedent were to describe the lighting conditions in this room and my present physiological and psychological state, then the final consequent would describe the "appearances" I am now sensing. The statement-form has four blanks, to be filled by terms describing four different sets of conditions or events. To the extent, therefore, to which we can keep any two of these sets of conditions constant and vary a third, we may be able to produce variations in the fourth.

The language we use to describe these variations is sometimes ambiguous or misleading; this fact is closely connected with the philosophical puzzles historically associated with the concept of *secondary quality*.

2. The word "blue" is sometimes used to designate a secondary quality of physical things. Occasionally it is used to designate the physical foundation of such a property or quality—the microscopic structure which a thing must have if it is to have the secondary quality *blue*. And frequently the word "blue" is used to designate a kind or species of appearing; a thing which may, or may not, have the secondary quality *blue* is then said to appear or to look blue. Many other adjectives are used, similarly, to designate either a secondary quality, a microscopic structure, or a way of appearing, or of sensing.[2] It is, perhaps, a typically philosophical error to confuse these uses.

Democritus said, of those "images" or "appearances" usually

---

[2] "Blue" is also used, occasionally, to designate light of a certain wave length—light which is reflected by things having the secondary quality *blue*. In *Sensation and Perception in the History of Experimental Psychology* (New York, 1952), E. G. Boring mentions still further uses of such terms (p. 131).

designated by such words as "sweet," "bitter," "warm," "cold,"
"red," and "black," (1) that they exist only when sensed by
some perceiver. We might express this proposition more generally by saying that nothing appears—in any way at all—unless it appears in some way *to* some living thing. From this
proposition Democritus evidently inferred (2) that no *un-*
perceived physical thing can be said to *be* sweet or bitter, warm
or cold, red or black. Other philosophers, believing that (2) is
false, have deduced that (1) is false. Having decided that
nature "holds within it the greenness of the trees, the song
of the birds, the warmth of the sun, the hardness of the chairs,
and the feel of the velvet," they have deduced, apparently,
that the appearances of these things continue to exist when
no one is sensing them.³ (This reasoning, if it were sound,
would constitute an objection to using the sensing terminology
which we recommended in the previous chapter. For the "grammar" of this terminology does not allow us to express the
proposition that there are appearances which exist when no
one is sensing them.)

Aristotle had seen that there is an ambiguity in saying that
(1), above, implies (2)—and hence, also, in saying that the
denial of (2) implies the denial of (1).

The earlier students of nature were mistaken in their view that
without sight there was no white or black, without taste no savour.
This statement of theirs is partly true, partly false. "Sense" and

---

³ The quotation is from A. N. Whitehead, *Concept of Nature* (Cambridge, 1920), p. 31. Contrast Locke: "He that will consider that the
same fire that at one distance produces in us the sensation of warmth, does
at a nearer approach produce in us the far different sansation of pain,
ought to bethink himself what reason he has to say, that this idea of
warmth which was produced in him by the fire, is actually in the fire, and
his idea of pain which the same fire produced in him the same way is
not in the fire" (*Essay*, bk. II, ch. viii, sec. 16). There is a good discussion
of the "pain argument" in D. J. B. Hawkins, *Criticism of Experience*, ch. ii.

"the sensible object" are ambiguous terms; i.e., they may denote either potentialities or actualities. The statement is true of the latter, false of the former. This ambiguity they wholly failed to notice.[4]

But Aristotle's own statement is more paradoxical than it needs to be. He points out, in effect, that a physical thing, at times when it is not being perceived, may yet have a "power" or "capacity" to stimulate the sensing of sound, color, flavor, or the like; for the thing may be such that, if certain conditions were to be realized, it *would* cause sensing to occur in these manners. And from this fact he concludes that such things, when they are not perceived, have *potential*, but not actual, sounds, colors, or flavors. But if we use the terms "sweet," "bitter," "warm," "cold," "red," and "black," as people often do use them, to designate secondary qualities, then we may say, less paradoxically, that unperceived things are sweet or bitter, warm or cold, red or black, provided only that they have the proper secondary qualities.[5] Spring leaves which have the secondary quality green are actually green and potentially red.

Sometimes green leaves look red. And when they do, people may say that what *looks* red is *really* green. But we should note that the redundant term "really" does not add any content to the sentences in which it occurs. Neither "Things that are really green may sometimes look red," "Things that are green may sometimes really look red," nor "Things that are green may sometimes look really red" adds anything to what is said by "Things that are green may sometimes look red."[6] The

---

[4] *De Anima*, III, ii, 426a; see also *Metaphysics*, IV, v, 1010b.

[5] Compare Thomas Reid, *Inquiry into the Human Mind*, ch. vi, secs. 4 and 5, and C. J. Ducasse, "On the Attributes of Material Things," *Journal of Philosophy*, XXXI (1934), 57–72.

[6] The American "New Realists" held that "things are just what they seem"—that the things we perceive are "precisely what they appear to be."

word "really" in "x is really green" serves only to stress the fact that "green" is not prefixed by "looks" or "appears," a purpose also served by writing "is" in italics.

And we must beware of saying that, when something green looks green, the thing and its appearance "have the same color." For "That looks green" does not mean that there is an appearance, or a way of appearing, which has the secondary quality *green*; that is, it does not mean that there is an appearance, or a way of appearing, which has "the power to produce" a green appearance.

Locke put the foregoing by saying that the ideas caused by secondary qualities are not "resemblances." [7]

3. Locke also said that the ideas caused by primary qualities *are* resemblances—"resemblances of something really existing in the objects themselves." [8] The *primary* qualities of things, it will be recalled, are "the bulk, figure, number, situation, and motion or rest of their solid parts." [9] Translating the terminology of "ideas" into that of "appearing," can we find any sense in which Locke's doctrine can be said to be true? This question, I believe, is more difficult than it may at first appear to be.

Let us consider three examples which will put Locke's view in a favorable light.

A man planning to take a photograph of the Pyramids may

See E. B. Holt, R. B. Perry, *et al.*, *The New Realism* (New York, 1912), p. 2. We need not accept this doctrine ("naive realism") if it is meant to imply: (i) that green things never look brown; (ii) that when green things look brown they are both green and brown; or (iii) that things may appear in certain ways without appearing *to* anyone in those ways.

[7] *Essay concerning Human Understanding*, bk. II, ch. viii, sec. 24.

[8] *Ibid.*, sec. 25.

[9] *Ibid.*, sec. 23.

want his photograph to convey some idea of their relative sizes and positions. And he may decide, therefore, that since one of the Pyramids falls between the others with respect to both size and location his photograph should be one in which the parts depicting the Pyramids are similarly related. Hence he finds a position for viewing the Pyramids from which one might say: "I am presented with an appearance containing three components, L, S, and M, such that: (i) M falls between the other two with respect to both size and position; (ii) each is an appearance of one of the Pyramids; and (iii) the Pyramid of which M is an appearance falls between the other Pyramids with respect to both size and position."

The opening phrase of *"La donna é mobile"*—A iterated three times, C, B flat, and G—exhibits an order such that, in one dimension or direction of that order, the fourth and sixth members are separated by the greatest interval and the first three fall between the fifth and the sixth. A person who has heard this phrase might say: "I have sensed six successive appearances which are related as are the six notes sung by the tenor—and as are the notes on his music and the grooves on the record."

A victim of double vision may look at one rectangular window and "seem to see" two windows, each one appearing rectangular. Realizing his limitation, he might say: "I sense two appearances which, in relation to the window that appears, are approximately the same in shape but are double in number."

It should be noted that the quotations included in these examples cannot be put in the sensing terminology we recommended in the previous chapter. Hence Locke would not accept our recommendation.

If the first two examples indicate that sometimes the "ideas

131

caused by primary qualities" are resemblances,[10] the third indicates that sometimes they are not. The appearances presented by the window differ from the window "in number." And if the man were to move to one side, he could obtain two appearances of the window, each of which differs from the window in shape. Conceding all of this, however, we wish to know merely whether things ever *can* be said to resemble the ways in which they appear.

The appear statements I have quoted in the three examples must be taken in their *noncomparative* sense, if Locke's view is true. The statement (1) "The window appears rectangular" must *not* be interpreted as saying merely, (2) "The window appears the way rectangular things would appear under optimum conditions." The word "rectangular"—according to Locke's view—has the same meaning in both (1) and (2); in (2) it applies to the window and in (1) it applies to the appearance of the window, or to the way in which the window appears. And similarly for the other examples; predicates which describe the primary qualities of physical things are also used to describe the ways in which those things appear.

I suggested in the previous chapter that the adjectives which follow the verb "appear" are *not* predicates qualifying an appearance or a way of appearing. According to what I said there, the adjective "rectangular" as it is used in "The window appears rectangular" is not a predicate attributing a characteristic to the way in which the window appears. The two words "appears rectangular" constitute a predicate which attributes a certain characteristic to the window. Similarly, "rectangular appearance" is to be compared, not with "rectangular window," but with "rectangular shape." The relation of *appearance* to

[10] Aristotle had noted, concerning primary qualities (the "common sensibles"), that "it is in respect of these that the greatest amount of sense-illusion is possible" (*De Anima*, III, iii, 428b).

132

rectangular in "The appearance is rectangular" is not that of subject to attribute.

Our three examples may tempt us to reject this doctrine and to say, with Locke, that the things we perceive may sometimes resemble the ways in which they appear to us—that some of the predicates designating the primary qualities of things may also be used, without ambiguity or change of meaning, to designate the ways in which some things appear. If we do agree with Locke, no one, I feel can show that we are mistaken.[11] But is there any good reason for agreeing with Locke?

The doctrine of the previous chapter, which we have contrasted with that of Locke, has the merit of greater economy and simplicity. When we ask about the way in which something appears, we are asking about one of the attributes—a relational attribute—of the *thing* that appears. But, according to our doctrine, we cannot ask about the attributes of the *way* in which the thing appears. For "the way in which the thing appears" does not designate a subject of attributes.

I know of one plausible argument for Locke's view—one which is associated with the doctrine of empiricism.

4. It is sometimes said that, before we can learn about the things that appear to us, we must learn about their appearances, about the ways in which they appear to us. One might say, for example, "Before we can know anything about the shapes of physical things, we know about the shapes of their appearances; before we can know whether any physical things are rectangles, we know that some of them look rectangular, that they present appearances which are rectangles; then, gradually, we learn to tell which physical things are rectangles." If this

---

[11] Bertrand Russell defends this view in *Human Knowledge*, pt. IV, chs. iii and iv, and pt. VI, ch. vi; compare his *Introduction to Mathematical Philosophy* (London, 1919), ch. vi.

appear statement were taken in its comparative sense, it would be contradictory, for it would imply: "Before we can know anything about rectangular physical things or whether there are such things, we know that some things look the way that rectangular physical things look under certain conditions." The statement, therefore, must be taken in its noncomparative sense. And it is one which cannot be true unless some of the predicates, describing the primary qualities of things, may also be used to describe the ways in which things appear.

A somewhat similar view might be taken of our knowledge of the secondary qualities of things, but with one significant difference. It is sometimes suggested that we first learn about the "colors of appearances" and that we subsequently learn about the colors of physical things; we first learn that certain appearances are red and we later learn that certain things are red. It would be in accord with this suggestion to say that we first apply "red" to appearances and later learn how to apply it to physical things.[12] It would not be plausible, however, to go on to say that "red" retains its original meaning when we apply it to physical things. For when we say that a physical thing is red, we may mean that it has the capacity to present a red appearance. Hence anyone accepting this account of the origins of our knowledge should say that "red," unlike "rec-

---

[12] The following dialogue occurs in bk. II of J. G. Fichte's *Vocation of Man:*

"*Spirit.* . . . Perhaps you have learned, by comparing the red or blue colours, the smooth or rough surfaces of objects *external to yourself* what you should experience within yourself as red or blue, sweet or rough?

"*I.* This is impossible; for my perception of objects proceeds from my perception of my own internal condition, and is determined by it—not the reverse. I first distinguish objects by distinguishing my own states of being. I can learn that this particular sensation is indicated by the arbitrary sign, red; and those by the signs, blue, smooth, rough . . ." (The Library of Liberal Arts ed. [New York, 1956], p. 39).

tangular," undergoes a change of meaning—or takes on a new meaning as one learns about the powers, or dispositions, of things.

It is no part of philosophy, as I conceive it, to speculate about the growth and origins of language or of knowledge. But if we are to retain our "adjectival" conception of appearing, we must be able to show, if only schematically, that our language habits and our knowledge need not have developed in the manner just described.

If there is any evidence for supposing that, genetically, our knowledge "begins with appearances," this evidence, I believe, may be interpreted in accordance with what I have said about appearing. Suppose we do find something that we are tempted to describe in this way: "At first, a red appearance is sufficient to elicit the predicate 'red' and a rectangular appearance is sufficient to elicit 'rectangular.' Then, later in the development of the individual, red and rectangular things elicit these predicates." What we would have found, I suggest, may be put as follows.

"We first use the thing-predicate 'red' in the way in which we later use such expressions as 'appears red' and 'looks red.' At first we say that a thing *is* red provided only that it looks red. Later, when we find out about lights and reflections and glasses, we become more selective and withhold 'red' from certain things which appear red and we apply 'red' to certain things which do not appear red. As the meaning of 'red' becomes more and more determinate, the expressions 'looks red' and 'appears red' come to take over the former, less discriminate uses of 'red.'

"At first, we say that a thing 'is rectangular' provided only that it meets the conditions we later describe as 'looking rectangular.' Then, as we become more discriminating, we revise our criteria. Some of the things that look rectangular are no longer called 'rectangular,' and some of the things that we call 'rectangular' need no longer look rectangular."

According to my suggestion, then, there is no reason to suppose that we first apply our predicates to appearances and later apply them to the things which present appearances. From the first, we apply our predicates to the things. But it may be that we first apply certain predicates "so-and-so" in the way in which we later apply the predicate "appears so-and-so." [13] If my suggestion is true, then we need not accept the view that there is a time when we attribute our predicates to the ways in which things appear. And if we need not accept this view, we need not accept Locke's view that the primary qualities of things are "resemblances."

I suggested in Chapter Four that it is a part of the doctrine of "empiricism" to hold that we cannot apply any predicate or adjective "so-and-so" until we know how to apply the expression "appears so-and-so." We cannot know how to apply "red" until we know how to apply "appears red" or "looks red." If this doctrine is taken to imply that we learn how to describe appearances or ways of sensing *before* we learn how to describe "external" physical things, then, according to my present suggestion, the doctrine is false. For when we first describe ways of appearing, we *are* describing the physical things that appear. All that a thing must do to merit the predicate "red," in this early use, is to *look* red. But the empirical doctrine *could* be taken to mean, simply, that we learn the

[13] A somewhat similar view is proposed by C. H. Whiteley, "Meaning and Ostensive Definition," *Mind*, LXV (1956), 332–335. What I have said above and what I have said about "empiricism" may be said to support K. R. Popper's criticisms of "inductivism." See his *Logik der Forschung* (Vienna, 1935) and "Three Views Concerning Human Knowledge" in *Contemporary British Philosophy*, 3d ser., H. D. Lewis ed. (London, 1956).

secondary-quality use of "red" *after* we have learned the use of a term which, in the early stage of our development, we used synonymously with our later use of "appears red." And if the empirical doctrine is taken in this second way, then, according to my suggestion, it is true.

There is another way in which "red" and other secondary-quality words may undergo a change of meaning as people learn more about the things to which such words apply. I suggested above that to be able to say of anything that it has a certain secondary quality is to be able to complete a statement of this sort: "If under . . . conditions the thing stimulates a perceiver who is . . . , then the perceiver will sense in a . . . manner." The best that most of us can do with the blanks in such a statement is to supply such words as "normal," "usual," or "ordinary." A thing is said to have the secondary quality *red* if in ordinary daylight it looks red to ordinary people—to people like ourselves. But a physicist or a psychologist, who knows more than we do about the conditions under which things look red, can replace "ordinary" and "usual" by more precise descriptions. And for such a person the secondary-quality word may come to have a more precise meaning than it has for the rest of us.

5.   The words we use to describe our feelings—our emotions, moods, and "feeling-tones"—are often used to describe the properties of things.

Shall we say an "agreeable degree of heat," or an "agreeable feeling" occasioned by the degree of heat? Either will do; and language would lose most of its esthetic and rhetorical value were we forbidden to project words primarily connoting our affections upon the objects by which the affections are aroused. The man is really hateful; the action really mean; the situation really tragic—all in themselves and quite apart from our opinion. We even go so far as to talk of a weary road, a giddy height, a jocund morning or a sullen sky.[14]

We may ask whether the road is "objectively" weary, or the degree of heat agreeable, or the sunset beautiful. And our answers should depend, in part, upon whether the adjectives "weary," "agreeable," and "beautiful" are to be taken as designating feelings or as designating properties of things.

Among the properties of a painting, for example, may be that of being able to cause certain perceivers to experience a melancholy feeling. If the painting is a good one, perhaps the experience is better described by saying that the painting has a melancholy flavor or tone. Thus, if we knew enough about "psychophysics," we could confirm statements of this sort:

> If under . . . conditions the painting stimulates a perceiver who is . . . the painting will have a melancholy tone for him.

Once we know the aesthetic properties of a thing, it would be an easy matter (if we were interested) to discover the microscopic "foundations" of these properties. And the feelings in question may be described—insofar as they are describable at all—by means of the sensing terminology discussed in the previous chapter.

There are, of course, important respects in which our feelings—or the feeling-tones of what we perceive—differ from what we have been calling "appearances." It may be that our feelings are more likely to vary with slight changes in our attitudes and our beliefs than are the appearances we sense. Hence the statements describing aesthetic properties may have to refer to many physiological and psychological conditions which

[14] William James, *Essays in Radical Empiricism* (New York, 1912), pp. 143–144.

are irrelevant to the sensing of appearances.[15] And therefore the presence of aesthetic properties in an object or situation may be less easy to ascertain than is the presence of "secondary qualities." But these complications, I believe, do not point to any important difference between the two types of property.

If we choose, we may also speak of the *ethical* or *moral* properties of things and events. We could define "good," or "valuable," in such a way that statements of the form "*x* is good," or "*x* is valuable," could be translated into statements of the following sort, where the blanks are replaced by terms which are "ethically neutral":

If under . . . conditions a perceiver who is . . . is stimulated in virtue of *x*, he will appraise *x* favorably.

I use the expression "appraise *x* favorably," instead of "morally approve of *x*" or "take *x* to be good," in order not to prejudge the question, discussed in Chapter Seven, whether such "appraisal" is true or false. And I use the expression "stimulated in virtue of *x*," instead of "*x* stimulates," in order to provide for the possibility that *x* is an event or state of affairs and not a physical thing.

If we say that charity is good or valuable, using "good" or "valuable" in the present sense, we would mean that whenever a certain type of perceiver is physically confronted with anyone's charitable act—say, under "normal" observation conditions—he will appraise the act favorably. A value statement of this sort does not differ in any philosophically interesting way from statements about the "secondary qualities" of things. If the philosophical terms "objective," "scientific," "factual," "descrip-

---

[15] Compare Alexius Meinong, *Über emotionale Präsentation* (Vienna, 1917); C. J. Ducasse, *Art, the Critics, and You* (New York, 1944), ch. iv; C. I. Lewis, *An Analysis of Knowledge and Valuation*, chs. xii and xiii; and Sören Halldén, *Emotive Propositions* (Stockholm, 1954).

tive," and their synonyms are applicable to such statements
as "This piece of tile is blue" and "It is more dangerous to go
by plane than by ship," they are also applicable to such statements as "That action is a good thing" and "It is better to
relieve the misery of many than to increase the pleasure of a
few"—*provided* that the ethical terms in the latter statements
are used in the property sense described above.

Have we found, then, a solution to the puzzles of Chapter
Seven? There we raised a question about ethical and epistemic
"appraisal" which we did not answer. We asked: Is such appraisal like believing, taking, and judging, in that it is either
true or false? Or is it, rather, like being amused, in that it is
neither true nor false? We asked similar questions about the
statements—for example, "That act is right"—in which such
appraisal may be expressed. Are these statements true or false?
And are they statements for which we can have evidence?

We may assign a property meaning, in the sense described
above, to "That act is right" and to the other statements we
discussed in Chapter Seven. But when these statements are
taken in their property sense, they no longer have the meaning they had in Chapter Seven. They become statements expressing our beliefs about certain causal properties of things;
they are no longer statements expressing our moral appraisal—
our moral beliefs or attitudes about these things.[16]

From the fact that value statements, in their property interpretation, are statements which are either true or false, it does
not follow, then, that our appraisals are either true or false. A
man who does *not* favorably appraise a certain object or event

---

[16] There are many moral and aesthetic terms which, in their ordinary use,
are ambiguous with respect to these two uses. There is a good discussion of
some of these terms ("A-words") in P. H. Nowell-Smith, *Ethics* (London,
1954), ch. vi. The "naturalistic fallacy" in ethics may take the form of an
equivocation with respect to these two uses; see R. M. Hare, *The Language
of Morals* (Oxford, 1952), ch. v.

may yet *believe* that the object or event meets the conditions of the property sense of "good." For he may concede that people of the sort required by the definition—normal people or (he might say) "average" people—do appraise it favorably. And a man who *does* favorably appraise a certain object or event may yet know that it does not have the property *good*— that people of the required sort do not appraise it favorably. If we interpret "good" in the above sense and if we continue to interpret "favorably appraise" as synonymous with the word "approve," as that word was intended in Chapter Seven, then we may say that to believe something to be good is *not* the same as to appraise it favorably. We cannot say, therefore, that what holds of statements which express our beliefs about *value* must also hold of statements which express our moral and epistemic *appraisals*.[17]

---

[17] "Valuation is always a matter of empirical knowledge. But what is right and what is just, can never be determined by empirical facts alone" (C. I. Lewis, *An Analysis of Knowledge and Valuation*, p. 554).

Ten

The Perception of Things

1. The verbs "perceive," "see," "hear," and "observe" are ordinarily used with one or the other of two types of grammatical object. We may say, "I see that a man is coming down the lane." Or we may say, "I see a man." In the first case, "see" takes a propositional clause as its grammatical object; in the second, it takes a noun. The objects of "hear," "perceive," and "observe" may, similarly, be either propositional or nonpropositional. "Taste" and "smell" may occasionally take propositional objects, but for the most part they are used nonpropositionally, with nouns or descriptive phrases.

In Chapter One, Section 1, I proposed a definition of the most important propositional use of "perceive." In the present chapter, I shall define nonpropositional uses of "perceive," "see," "hear," and a number of other perception words. Given these definitions one could, I believe, define all other important uses of perception words. I shall also discuss certain philosophical questions concerning the relations between the propositional and nonpropositional senses of these words.

The Perception of Things

2. We will find, if I am not mistaken, that "S perceives x," in one familiar nonpropositional use, means the same as "x *appears* in some way to S." We have discussed at length the grammatical predicate of the locution "x appears so-and-so"; let us now consider its subject.

In Chapter Eight, I suggested this definition of *appear*:

> "x appears . . . to S" means that S senses . . . with respect to x.

The term "sense," I there said, may be used for describing many types of experience other than that of "being appeared to"; hence there is a theoretical advantage in defining "appear" in terms of "sense." But I have not yet said what it is to sense *with respect to* an object. I shall now try to reformulate our definition of "appear" in such a way that the phrase "with respect to" is replaced by *causal* terms.

Our problem is best seen, I think, if we begin with an oversimplified definition of "appear" and then note the respects in which our definition needs to be modified.

Let us consider, first, the following definition:

> "x appears . . . to S" means that x causes S to sense. . . .

This definition is quite obviously too broad. If we take the expression "x causes S to sense" to mean merely that x is a *causal condition* of S's sensing, then according to the above definition we must say, of all those physical and psychological conditions necessary to being alive and conscious, that *they* appear to us whenever we sense in any way. For one would not sense in any way at all unless, for example, one had sense organs and a nervous system. But we do not wish to say that, whenever anyone senses in a certain way, his sense organs and nervous system *appear* to him in that particular way.

Shall we say, then, that the things that *appear* are always external stimuli, things that act upon the receptors of the perceiving subject? We might modify our definition in this way:

"*x* appears . . . to S" means that *x* stimulates the receptors of S and that, in consequence, S senses. . . .

But our definition remains too broad. Light waves and sound waves may stimulate the receptors of S and cause him to sense in certain ways. But we do not wish to say that the light waves or sound waves thereby *appear* to S in those ways or in any other ways.

To exclude such "improper" objects, let us introduce the concept of a *proper stimulus* and then specify that what appears to S must be something which is a proper stimulus of S.

We may say that *x* is a proper *visual* stimulus for S provided (i) that light transmitted from *x* stimulates a visual receptor of S and (ii) that this light, after being transmitted from *x* and before reaching the visual receptors of S, is not reflected. When we look at the moon at night, our eyes are stimulated by light from the sun; the proper stimulus, however, is the moon and neither the light nor the sun.

We may say that *x* is a proper *auditory* stimulus for S provided that soundwaves transmitted from *x* stimulate an auditory receptor of S. The proper auditory stimulus is thus neither the sound waves nor the medium through which they are transmitted, but the vibrating object that transmits them. The proper *olfactory* stimuli are odoriferous particles which stimulate the olfactory receptors; those of *taste* are the substances that enter and stimulate the taste buds; and those of *touch* are whatever, by pushing or pulling the skin, stimulates the touch spots. For other types of kinesthetic sensation it is enough, I think, to say that any kinesthetic stimulus is a "proper stimulus."

144

The Perception of Things

Let us say generally, then, that a *proper stimulus* is a stimulus of any one of the types we have just described.[1] We might now modify our definition of "appear" in this way:

"x appears . . . to S" means that, as a consequence of x being a proper stimulus of S, S senses. . . .

With this definition, we no longer have to say that light waves and sound waves are included among the things that appear. And if a man's sense organs are stimulated artificially or improperly—if, say, an electrode or the blow of another man's fist causes him to "see stars"—the stimulus need not be described as something that appears. But our definition is still too broad.

We must find a way of ruling out those *images* which may be called up as the effect of some proper stimulus x but which we do not wish to call appearances of x. A traveler, on looking out of a railroad car, sees something reminding him of an earlier trip and, in consequence, he visualizes a certain strip of land along the Pacific ocean. In so doing, he may "sense bluely" despite the fact that none of the things he sees *appears* blue to him. The things he sees are proper stimuli, and it is because of them that he "senses bluely." Hence, according to our definition above, we may say, falsely, that the things that stimulate his eyes as he looks out the window appear blue. We must find a way, therefore, of distinguishing the "impression" from the mere "idea."

For the empirical theories of Berkeley, Hume, and Kant, it was essential to distinguish between impression and idea without making any reference to the external sources of stimulation. Tending to accept both forms of the doctrine that our knowl-

---

[1] In psychological literature, the term "stimulus object" is sometimes used to designate a proper stimulus.

edge "begins with appearances" (see Chapter Six, Sections 1 and 2, and Chapter Nine, Section 4), these philosophers sought to find some "internal" mark by means of which the perceiver could distinguish between the appearances of things and the imagery which sometimes accompanies these appearances. Berkeley said, it may be recalled, that

the ideas of sense are more strong, lively, and distinct than those of the imagination; they have likewise a steadiness, order, and coherence, and are not excited at random, as those which are the effects of human wills often are, but in a regular train or series, the admirable connexion whereof sufficiently testifies the wisdom and benevolence of its Author.[2]

The last of these marks—the *regularity* which distinguishes the impressions of sense from the ideas of the imagination—will enable us, I think, to complete our definition of "appearing." But, unlike Berkeley, Hume, and Kant, I believe that this regularity can be described only by referring to certain properties of the stimulus.[3]

In our example of the traveler who visualizes the sights of an earlier trip as he looks out the window, we have an idea and

---

[2] George Berkeley, *Principles of Human Knowledge*, sec. 46.

[3] I shall criticize some of the details of Berkeley's doctrine in the Appendix. Hume's discussion of the question "What causes induce us to believe in the existence of body?" (see *Treatise of Human Nature*, bk. I, pt. IV, sec. 2) and Kant's "transcendental doctrine of judgment" may be looked upon, I think, as attempts to refine upon Berkeley's criteria. The following quotation expresses the essence of Kant's doctrine: "If we enquire what new character *relation to an object* confers upon our representations, what dignity they thereby acquire, we find that it results only in subjecting the representations to a rule, and so in necessitating us to connect them in some one specific manner. . . ." (*The Critique of Pure Reason*, B 242; Norman Kemp Smith ed.). *Hume's Theory of the External World* (Oxford, 1940), by H. H. Price, and *Kant's Theory of Knowledge* (Oxford, 1909), by H. A. Prichard, are excellent discussions of these attempts.

an impression—an image and an appearance—each of which is dependent upon proper stimuli. It was in part because of the secondary qualities of the things our traveler was looking at that they *appeared* in the way in which they did appear— and had they not appeared in that particular way, he would not have visualized the sights of his earlier trip. Yet the impression is connected with the stimulus in a way in which the image is not.

If our traveler is a commuter who occupies the same seat each day and if he is in the habit of looking out, then the things along the track will appear in approximately the same way each day and in the same order. But the ways in which he imagines will vary with each trip. Our impressions, unlike our mere ideas or images, will vary systematically with variations in the proper stimuli.

Merely by making systematic changes in a proper stimulus and, so far as possible, keeping all other conditions constant, a "psychophysical" experimenter can produce systematic changes in the way in which his subject senses. By turning a dial, he can make an auditory stimulus sound high, then low, then somewhere in between, then low again, and then high again. Merely by changing the illumination, he can make similar systematic changes in the way in which a visual stimulus will appear. But he cannot readily produce systematic variations in the imagery of his subjects; to make his subject call up one image, then a second, then the first again, and so on, it is usually necessary for him to do something more than turn a dial.

Let us consider, then, the following modification of our definition of "appear":

"x appears . . . to S" means: (i) as a consequence of x being a proper stimulus of S, S senses . . . ; and (ii) in sensing . . . . , S senses in a way which may be made to vary concomitantly with variations in x.

I believe we need only one slight modification.

A skilled experimenter may, on occasion, achieve considerable control over his subject's imagery. By saying the right things or giving the right instructions, a hypnotist may be able to produce a stream of ideas or images which, for a while at least, will vary concomitantly with the changes in the sound of his voice. Our definition, as it now stands, would require us to say that the subject's stream of imagery is a way in which the *experimenter* appears.

If the subject's *imagery* may, on occasion, be made a function of changes in a proper stimulus, these changes must have a degree of complexity which cannot be made a function merely of the *degree* of stimulation. The experimenter must speak the language of his subject; or he must make considerable use of information about the subject's background and his present physiological and psychological state. But the way in which the proper stimulus *appears* will vary with changes of a much simpler sort.

To change the way in which the stimulus object appears, it is enough to change the degree—or intensity—of the stimulation. To make the stimulus object look different, we have only to increase the amount of light it reflects; to make it sound different, we have only to increase the volume of sound; and analogously for the other types of stimulus. The way in which an object appears may be made a function solely of the amount of energy in the stimulation it causes; in short, it may be made a function of the stimulus energy it produces. Let us consider, then, the possibility of defining "appear" in this general way:

"x *appears* . . . to S" means: (i) as a consequence of x being a proper stimulus of S, S senses . . . ; and (ii) in sensing . . . , S senses in a way that is functionally dependent upon the stimulus energy produced in S by x.

If this type of definition is satisfactory, as I believe it is, then we may say that "appear" is definable in terms of "sensing" and certain causal concepts of physics and physiology.[4]

3. We may now define the simplest of the nonpropositional senses of "perceive":

"S *perceives x*" means: x appears in some way to S.

The locution "S perceives x" in this, the most simple of its senses, may thus be thought of as one way of expressing the converse of "x appears in some way to S."

Corresponding senses of "see," "hear," "smell," "taste," and "touch" may be defined by making use of the *definiens* of our definition of "appear," above, adding a reference to the type of proper stimulus involved. For example, we may define the simplest of the nonpropositional senses of "see" in this way:

"S *sees x*" means that, as a consequence of x being a proper *visual* stimulus of S, S senses in a way that is functionally dependent upon the stimulus energy produced in S by x.

We may now say that an object is *in view* provided only that the subject is in a position where he can readily see the object.

Similar definitions may be provided for "hear," "smell," "taste," and "touch." And we may say of a man that he "is aware of" or "feels" a certain part of his body, in the nonpropositional senses of "is aware of" and "feels," provided only that he senses in some way as a result of kinesthetic stimulation in that part of his body.

---

[4] The definition presupposes, of course, that we have an adequate analysis of *functional dependence* and *causation*; my own views on the latter concepts may be found in "Law Statements and Counterfactual Inference," *Analysis*, XV (1955), 97–105.

Defining nonpropositional uses of perception words in this way, we need not accept the thesis, proposed by some writers on science, that what people perceive are light waves, sound waves, retinal images, parts of the brain, or ways of appearing.

I have said that such definitions are concerned with the simplest of the nonpropositional senses of the perception words defined. Perhaps we would hesitate to apply any of these words, even nonpropositionally, unless we believed that still another condition was fulfilled. Perhaps we would not want to say that a man *sees* an object x unless, in addition to sensing in the required way, the man also *took* the object x to *be* something. As we shall note in more detail below, there is no paradox involved in saying that a man *sees* a dog without taking what he sees to *be* a dog. It may be, however, that we would hesitate to say that he sees a dog if he didn't take it to be anything at all. To make our definitions adequate to this felt requirement, we have only to add the qualification:

and S takes x to have some characteristic.

Using perception words in the way they are defined here, we must say that there are people who perceive things, who see, hear, feel, or touch them, without *knowing* that they are perceiving anything, without knowing that they are seeing, hearing, feeling, or touching anything. For there are people who perceive things without knowing anything about the physical processes in terms of which we have defined the nonpropositional senses of perception words. Thus we could say, with Leibniz, that *apperception* is not given to all who have *perception*.[5] People who do not know that they are perceiving any-

---

[5] "Thus it is well to make distinction between *perception*, which is the inner state of the Monad representing outer things, and *apperception*, which is *consciousness* or the reflective knowledge of this inner state, and which is not given to all souls nor to the same soul at all times" (G. W. Leibniz,

thing may yet *say* that they do. They may say that they see, hear, feel, or touch things, but, in so saying, they use perception words in ways other than those defined here. If we wished our definitions to be adequate to their uses, we could still define such locutions as "S perceives x" in terms of "x appears in some way to S"; but we would replace the definition of "x appears in some way to S," which we finally settled upon, with one of the simpler definitions we had rejected.[6]

4. When a perception verb is used, nonpropositionally, with a grammatical object, the grammatical object designates something that is *appearing* in some way to the perceiver. If a man can be said to see a boat, for example, then the boat is appearing to him in some way. Hence, from the statement

(1) He sees a boat

we may infer

(2) A boat appears in some way to him.

And, if we choose, we may transform our conclusion as

(3) A boat presents him with an appearance.

But it would be fallacious then to infer

(4) He sees an appearance.

Let us refer to the inference of (4), from (1), (2), or (3), as an instance of the *sense-datum fallacy*.[7] One commits this fal-

---

"The Principles of Nature and Grace," sec. 4; in J. E. Erdmann, ed., *Leibnitii Opera Philosophica* [Berlin, 1840], p. 715).

[6] The above serves to illustrate "the evolution of concepts" in the development of the individual. Compare V. F. Lenzen on "successive definition," in *Procedures of Empirical Science* (International Encyclopedia of Unified Science, vol. I, no. 5 [Chicago, 1938]), and Arthur Pap, *The A Priori in Physical Theory* (New York, 1946). What we said about secondary-quality words in Chapter Nine, Section 4, provides another illustration of this process.

[7] H. A. Prichard used the expression "sense-datum fallacy" with a similar

lacy if, from a premise of the form "S perceives a . . . which appears . . . to him," one infers a conclusion of the form "S perceives an appearance which is. . . ." I use the word "fallacy" because (4) does not follow from (1), (2), and (3) and because, I believe, there is no true premise which, when conjoined with (1), (2), and (3), will yield (4) as a conclusion.[8]

Once the sense-datum fallacy has been committed, other mistakes are likely to follow. Perhaps the worst of these—illustrated in terms of our example—is the tendency to infer from (4) the contradictory of (1); namely,

(5) He does not see a boat.

Are there any acceptable premises which, when conjoined with (1), (2), and (3), will yield (4)? Sometimes, I think, philosophers and psychologists tend to reason in this way. Preferring the sense-datum terminology of (3) to the appearing terminology of (2), they note that the sensing of appearances is an indispensible condition of perceiving physical things; that is to say, they note that people wouldn't perceive things unless the things took on appearances for them. They then note that the sensing of appearances, unlike the states of "external" physi-

---

intent, I believe, but he described the fallacy in quite different terms. According to him, the fallacy consists in "thinking of perceiving as a kind of knowing" (*Knowledge and Perception* [Oxford, 1950], p. 213); I believe that he interpreted his term "perceiving" as I have interpreted "sensing" and that he described what I have called "perceiving" as one type of knowing. Gilbert Ryle's criticism of "the sense-datum theory," in *The Concept of Mind*, and Martin Lean's criticism of "the sensum theory," in *Sense-Perception and Matter* (London, 1953), also concern the sense-datum fallacy. See also P. Coffey, *Epistemology or the Theory of Knowledge*, II, 177 ff., and R. W. Sellars, "Realism, Naturalism, and Humanism," in G. P. Adams and W. P. Montague, eds., *Contemporary American Philosophy*, vol. II (New York, 1930).

[8] Indeed we have noted in Chapter Eight that it is even a mistake to infer "S senses an appearance which is . . ." from "x appears . . . to S."

cal things, takes place only as the effect of physiological and psychological processes. And, thirdly, they note that, often at least, a perceiver can find out what kind of appearances he is sensing—can know how things appear. Appealing to these facts, they then infer that statements such as (4) and (5) are true. Yet if we add a description of these facts, in all their relevant detail, to statements (1), (2), and (3), we still lack the premises needed to establish either (4) or (5).

The belief that people perceive only appearances or that they cannot perceive physical things often results from what seem to be philosophical paradoxes. For example, when we learn about the velocity of light and about the distances of the stars we see at night, we may begin to wonder whether we do see the stars we think we see. And when we are told that stars sometimes disrupt and become extinct and that possibly some of those we see tonight ceased to exist hundreds of years ago, we may feel that there is some paradox involved in supposing that we can perceive anything at all. But the paradox arises only because we tend to assume, until we are taught otherwise, that any event or state of affairs we perceive must exist or occur simultaneously with our perception of it. We tend to assume, more generally, that S can perceive a at t only if a exists at t. If we combine this assumption with what we now know about the finite velocity of sound and light, perhaps we can derive the conclusion that no one perceives any of the things he thinks he perceives. But to assume that S can perceive a at t only if a exists at t is no more reasonable than to assume that S can receive or reflect light from a at t only if a exists at t. The perception of a star that is now extinct should be no more paradoxical than the action of such a star on a photographic plate or its reflection in the water.

Some philosophers might put the foregoing by saying that, properly speaking, we perceive only certain *parts* of things and that the "temporal parts" we perceive of things always precede our perception of them. But the suggestion that we perceive only certain parts of things leads to still another paradox.

Descartes remarks, in the second of his *Meditations*, that if he were to look into the street where men are walking by, "the terms of ordinary language" might mislead him into saying that he sees men. "Nevertheless what do I see from this window except hats and cloaks which might cover automata? But I judge that they are men, and thus I comprehend, solely by the faculty of judgment which resides in my mind, that which I believed I saw with my eyes." But why not say that he sees men who are wearing hats and cloaks? Descartes's reasoning, apparently, is this: he does not see faces (let us suppose), and he does not see what is covered by the hats or the cloaks; hence (he concludes) he sees only hats and cloaks, not people wearing hats and cloaks. And if he were to continue with this reasoning, he might be led to say, even more strictly, that he does not see the hats or the cloaks. For he does not see the insides of the hats and cloaks; he does not see the sides which face away from him; nor does he even see all of the threads on those sides which do face him. Hence, by reasoning similar to the above, he might conclude that what he sees are at best certain *parts* of the surfaces of the outer parts of one of the sides of the hats and of the cloaks.[9] The next step in this reasoning would be to conclude: "Indeed, there is no part even of the outer surfaces which I see; for, with respect to any such part, there is, surely, some part of *it* which I do not see. What I see, therefore, cannot be a part of any physical things." [10]

---

[9] C. D. Broad reasons somewhat this way in *The Mind and Its Place in Nature* (London, 1925), pp. 149–150. Compare Martin Lean's criticism of Broad in *Sense-Perception and Matter*, pp. 65 ff.

[10] Note that this way of trying to show that we don't perceive what we ordinarily think we perceive differs from the courtroom technique discussed in Chapter Six, Section 5.

The Perception of Things

The mistake involved in this reasoning may be seen, I think, if we consider certain points about the "grammar" of "see" and of other perception words.

The locution "S sees x" should not be taken to imply "S sees every part of x." In this respect the verb "see" is unlike the verbs "carry," "own," and "contain." A truck cannot carry a box without carrying every part of it; a man cannot own a piece of land unless he owns every part of it; and any piece of land that contains a garden contains every part of the garden.[11] The grammar of "see" is more like that of "hit," "destroy," and "inhabit." An automobile may hit a truck without hitting every part of the truck; a bomb may destroy a cathedral without destroying every part of the cathedral; and a philosopher may inhabit Peru without inhabiting every part of Peru. And if "S sees x" does not imply "S sees every part of x," then "it is false that S sees all of the parts of x" does not imply "S does not see x." [12]

Our other perception words—"perceive," "hear," "smell,"

---

[11] Compare what H. S. Leonard and Nelson Goodman say about "dissective" and "expansive" predicates in "The Calculus of Individuals and Its Uses," *Journal of Symbolic Logic*, V (1940), especially 54–55. In Goodman's *Structure of Appearance* (Cambridge, Mass., 1951), the following definitions are proposed (pp. 48–49): "A one-place predicate is said to be *dissective* if it is satisfied by every part of every individual that satisfies it"; "a one-place predicate is *expansive* if it is satisfied by everything that has a part satisfying it." Compare also H. Hudson, "People and Part-Whole Talk," *Analysis*, XV (1955), 90–93.

[12] May we say, more strongly, that "S sees some but not all of the parts of x" *does* imply "S sees x"? The answer, I think, is unclear. The following two points are relevant. (i) It is true that, in seeing one soldier, we don't see the platoon, and in seeing the North Star, we don't thereby see the Little Dipper. But the relation of soldier to platoon, like that of star to constellation, is a relation of member to class rather than one of part to whole. (ii) I have noted above that "see" is like "destroy." A bomb may destroy a part of the cathedral—say, a small part of the roof—without destroying the cathedral.

"taste," "touch," "feel"—are like "see." The locution "S perceives *x*," for example, does not imply "S perceives every part of *x*." And the locution "S perceives some but not every part of *x*" does not imply "S does not perceive *x*." And so on analogously for the other perception words.

Descartes, in the reasoning I have attributed to him, seems to have overlooked these points. For he notes that, whenever we think we see something, there will be parts of that thing that we don't see; and then he infers that we cannot properly be said to see the thing at all. This mistake is comparable to saying: "Since the philosopher lives in some but not in all parts of Peru, he cannot properly be said to live in Peru at all" or "Since there are parts of the roast which the butcher didn't cut, therefore he didn't really cut the roast."

It is also misleading to say, as Moore does in *Some Main Problems of Philosophy*, that "whenever we talk roughly of seeing any object, it is true that, in another and stricter sense of the word *see*, we only see *a part of it*." [13] This is like saying, "whenever we talk roughly about a philosopher living in Peru, it is true that in another and stricter sense of the word 'in,' the philosopher lives, not in Peru, but in only a part of Peru."

5. The belief that what we perceive are the *appearances* of things sometimes leads philosophers to say that we *take* appearances *to be* the things we would ordinarily be said to perceive. We are said to "identify" the appearance with the thing that is appearing, thus unwittingly taking one thing to be another. Perception is then said to have an "*ersatz* character," to be a "*mis*taking," an "illusion" and a "sham"—for the perceiver *mis*takes the appearance for the thing that stimulates it.[14]

---

[13] G. E. Moore, *Some Main Problems of Philosophy* (London, 1953), p. 34.

[14] Compare H. H. Price, *Perception*, p. 169, and Prichard, *Knowledge and*

The Perception of Things

Ordinarily, we would not use the word "mistake" unless we thought that the man's (ostensible) perception was "unveridical" or that he was a victim of hallucination. A man might be said to mistake a clump of trees, say, for a house. In this case, it could be said that *what* he perceives is a clump of trees and that he erroneously takes this clump of trees to be a house. But according to the philosophical view I have mentioned, even when the man would be said to take something *veridically* to be a house, (i) what he *perceives* is merely an appearance and (ii) he *mistakes* this appearance for a house.

If what I have said is true, we have found no reason for asserting (i). The object of the perception—what the man perceives—is the house and not the appearance of the house. Hence, we have no ground for asserting (ii). And, in fact, it is very difficult to catch anyone in such a "mistake"—to find anyone being taken in by any such "sham." We have only to ask our perceiver, for example, whether he thinks it's the house, or the appearance of the house, that is appearing to him.

Some of the American "Critical Realists" expressed a similar philosophical view, using the term "substitute" instead of "mistake." Roy Wood Sellars said of appearances that "these sensible characters which are open to inspection and so readily taken to be literal aspects, surfaces, and inherent qualities of physical things are *subjective substitutes* for the corresponding parts of the physical world." [15] But the word "substitute," it

---

Perception, pp. 52, 62. Hippolyte Taine used the term "veridical hallucination" in this context. Price has noted that "when Prichard discussed his theory with his colleagues in Oxford, they would often object that normal perception is not mistaking in the sense in which illusory perception is, and they would urge him to admit that some perceptual 'mistakings' are at any rate *less* mistaken than others" (review of Prichard, *op. cit.*, in *Mind*, LX [1951], 117).

[15] "Knowledge and Its Categories," p. 191, included in Durant Drake, *et al.*, *Essays in Critical Realism* (New York, 1920). Despite the fact that

seems to me, is no better than "mistake." Ordinarily if we were to say that a man has *substituted* something A for something else B, we would mean: that he has removed B and replaced it by A; or that he responds to A as he once responded to B; or that, when A is more readily available than B, he uses A, as next best, in the way he would like to use B. But we do not want to say that the perceiver has removed the object and replaced it by the appearance or that he responds to the appearance as he once responded to the object. And we have found no reason for supposing that physical things are not available to be perceived.

It is sometimes said that to perceive something is to "make an inference" or to "frame a hypothesis"—an inference or hypothesis about the causal conditions of sensing. To perceive a man walking, according to this "inferential theory," is to "infer" or "frame the hypothesis" that one's sensory experience has been stimulated by a man walking. I have said that *what* one perceives is indeed the proper stimulus of one's sensory experience. But surely no perceiver, on opening his eyes in the morning, can be said to "infer" that he is surrounded by familiar objects or to "frame the hypothesis" that these objects stimulate the appearances he is sensing. Perceiving no more consists in deducing the causes of sensing than reading consists in deducing the causes of ink marks.

If we do use the words "inference" and "hypothesis" in this context, we cannot take them in their ordinary sense—in the

---

Sellars speaks of appearances as "substitutes," his essay is a useful criticism of the "sense-datum fallacy." Holding that some appearances "resemble" the things that stimulate them (see Section 3 of the previous chapter), Sellars was able to say that these "substitutes" have a "sort of revelatory identity with the object" (p. 200). C. A. Strong's view in "On the Nature of the Datum," also included in the *Essays in Critical Realism*, was similar; but he later revised it in several important respects.

sense in which a physician, studying symptoms, may be said to "make an inference" or "frame a hypothesis" about the disorders of his patient. Use of the technical psychological terms "unconscious inference" and "interpretation," in this context, serves only to obscure the fact that perceiving is *not* an inference, in the ordinary sense of the word "inference." [16]

Nor should we say that the perceiver takes an appearance to be a sign of the object or—what is even more inaccurate—that he takes it to be a kind of *picture*, or reproduction of the object. When writers on philosophy and popular science say that what people perceive are "pictures" or other "representatives" of things, they have apparently deduced this conclusion from the propositions (i) that what people perceive are appearances and (ii) that appearances may be "resemblances of something really existing in the objects themselves." But according to what I have said, the first of these premises is a result of the sense-datum fallacy and is clearly false; and the second is either false or nonsense.

Using "perceive" in its propositional sense, I said in Chapter Six that, whenever a man perceives something to have some characteristic and thus takes it to have that characteristic, he accepts—or assumes—certain propositions about sensing, or "being appeared to." If he takes something to be a row of trees, then, according to my suggestion, he is sensing in a certain way; he assumes, with respect to one of the ways he is sensing, that, if he were not sensing in that way, he would not be perceiving a tree. Moreover, he assumes that, if we were to *act* in certain ways, he would sense in still other ways —ways in which he would not sense if he were not now

---

[16] There is an excellent criticism of "inferential theories" of perception in D. J. B. Hawkins, *Criticism of Experience* (London, 1945), ch. vi. See also P. G. Winch, "The Notion of 'Suggestion' in Thomas Reid's Theory of Perception," *Philosophical Quarterly*, III (1953), 327–341.

perceiving a tree. In saying that he assumes or accepts these propositions, I do not mean that they are the object of deliberate or conscious inference. In saying that he assumes or accepts them, I mean merely that, if he were to learn that they are false, he would be surprised and would then set out, deliberately and consciously, to revise his store of beliefs.

Ordinarily a perceiver may not notice the way in which the object of his perception happens to be appearing. If we ask him to tell us about what it is that he is perceiving, he will not reply by telling us how the things he is perceiving happen to appear to him. And subsequently he will find it easier to remember *what* it was that he perceived than to remember *how* it was that the objects of his perception happened to look, or otherwise appear, to him. He may be able to recall that he saw a square garden, for example, without being able to recall whether it looked diamond-shaped or rectangular. It is here, perhaps, that the familiar analogy between perception and language is most instructive. Thus one might say, in reporting a conversation, "I don't recall the exact words he used, but I remember his telling me that the climate there is not very pleasant in the winter." One recalls, not the details of the language, but rather what it is that was conveyed. Such points as these are frequently put in metaphors. It is often said, for example, that the object of perception "transcends" the "vehicle" of perception. Reid said that the appearance is likely to "hide itself" behind the shadow of the object perceived and "pass through the mind unobserved." [17] And some writers have used the metaphor of "transparency": one perceives the ob-

---

[17] Thomas Reid, *An Inquiry into the Human Mind*, ch. v, secs. 2 and 8. Compare Roderick Firth's discussion of these facts in "Sense Data and the Percept Theory," *Mind*, LVIII (1949), 434–465. Firth challenges us to show that we *are* appeared to on such occasions. I am convinced that we are, but it would be difficult to show that we are.

ject "through" the sensible appearance.[18] But, I suggest, to say of a man that he *does not notice* the way he is appeared to is to say that, although he is appeared to in that way, it is false that he believes—that he accepts the proposition—that he is appeared to in that way. (It is essential to our theory of evidence that we do not, at this point, confuse the locutions "It is false that S accepts *h*" and "S accepts non-*h*").

There are times when appearances play a more important role than they do in ordinary perception. We have seen that people can be led to *defend* their perceptual statements by making statements about the way in which the object of their perception appears. If an appearance is painful, or pleasurable, or aesthetically significant, it may be of more interest than the object which appears and hence it is no longer "transparent." [19] The appearance may also be of interest when the conditions of observation are under investigation. One's concern in the optometrist's shop is not with what the particular letters on the chart may happen to be, but with the way in which they appear. The man in charge of the stage lighting will be concerned not with the actual colors of the setting, but with the way in which they appear under certain conditions. And philosophers and psychologists, studying perception, may be concerned with the nature of the appearances rather than with the objects which appear. The peculiar talent of the psychologist, according to Wundt and Titchener and their followers, is his skill in at-

---

[18] Compare Edmund Husserl, *Logische Untersuchungen*, vol. II, pt. ii, pp. 237–238.

[19] Compare Arthur Schopenhauer: "Those sensations which principally serve for the objective comprehension of the external world must in themselves be neither agreeable nor disagreeable. This really means that they must leave the will entirely unaffected. Otherwise the sensation *itself* would attract our attention . . ." (*The World as Will and Idea* [tr. by R. G. Haldane and John Kemp], II, 193; see also 189–190). Compare in addition Reid's *Essays on the Intellectual Powers*, ch. v, sec. 2.

tending to the appearance rather than to the object of perception; and it is difficult to attain this skill, since in order to
do so one must overcome the natural habit of "looking
through" the appearance.[20]

6. Corresponding to the propositional and nonpropositional
senses of *perceiving,* a distinction may be made between two
kinds of *deception* or *error.*

What is usually called "unveridical" perceiving—what we
might call "*mis*taking"—is an error which may be contrasted
with perceiving, in the propositional sense of "perceiving." But
hallucination, in one of its extreme forms, is an error, or a type
of deception, which may be contrasted with perceiving, in *both*
the propositional and the nonpropositional senses of "perceive."

A victim of hallucination may think he sees an animal—
may *take* something to be an animal—at a time when *nothing*
is appearing to him. He may be sensing in one of the ways he
would sense if he were looking at an animal, but he is not
sensing "with respect to" anything—his experience is not the
result of any proper stimulus. His error, therefore, is not merely
a matter of *mis*taking. It is not merely a matter of taking the
proper stimulus to have some characteristic that it does not
have; for there is *no* proper stimulus. We allow ourselves to say
that he "takes something" to be an animal; but strictly there is no
"something" there.[21] Perhaps we could say that his error is that

---

[20] Reid says that this habit, which "has been gathering strength ever since
we began to think," is one "the usefulness of which, in common life, atones
for the difficulty it creates to the philosopher" (*An Inquiry into the Human
Mind,* ch. v, sec. 2). According to what I suggested in the previous chapter
(Section 4), we do not even "begin" by considering appearances.

[21] Note that I defined "S takes x to be f" (Chapter Six, Section 3) in
terms of "S is appeared to (senses) in a certain way" and *not* in terms of
"S is appeared to (senses) in a certain way *with respect to* something" or

of assuming that there *is* something which is appearing. (Even if we know that the source of his hallucination was a drug, or some organic defect, we are not tempted to say that it was the drug or the organic defect which appeared to him.) According to Reid, mistakes of this sort—which are commonly made only "in a delirium or in madness"—are the only mistakes properly called "deceptions of sense." [22]

The linguistic counterpart of this extreme form of hallucination is what might be called "mistaken indication." Whenever we perceive anything, we can express our perception in statements wherein the things perceived are designated—or indicated —by demonstrative terms alone. If we can say, "That boat looks green," we may reformulate our statement as "That is (identical with) a boat and looks green," using "that" purely demonstratively to indicate the thing which, as it happens, we have taken to be a boat and which looks green. Even if we use the terminology of "appearance," saying, "That boat takes on a green appearance," the demonstrative term indicates, not the appearance, but the thing we have taken to be a boat.[23] When the victim of hallucination uses a demonstrative term, saying, "That is a rat," the term "that" may seem to indicate, or pur-

---

"Something appears in a certain way to S." The statement "S takes something to be red," given our definition of "taking," does *not* entail "Something is appearing in some way to S." If it did, then sensibly-taking, contrary to our theory of evidence (Chapter Six, Section 5), would no longer fulfill our second condition for a mark of evidence (Chapter Three, Section 3); the victim of hallucination would be quite capable of believing falsely that something is appearing to him (in the sense of "appear" defined in the present chapter), and therefore he would be quite capable of believing falsely that he was taking something to be red.

[22] Reid, *Essays on the Intellectual Powers*, Essay II, ch. xiii.

[23] Compare Husserl, *op. cit.*, vol. II, pt. II, especially pp. 14–16; Price, *Perception*, ch. vi; A. N. Whitehead, "Indication, Classes, Numbers, Validation," in *Essays in Science and Philosophy* (New York, 1947), especially pp. 313–314.

port to indicate, but actually it indicates nothing.[24] It cannot indicate the proper stimulus—the thing that appears—because, in this instance, there is no proper stimulus; nothing appears. But the man who mistakes a pile of rocks for a house and says, "That is a house," does not make a mistake of indication, for his word "that" does indicate something—it indicates the thing that appears.

7. Let us consider, finally, some of the more interesting relations holding between the propositional and nonpropositional uses of perception words.

The statement "Jones saw that a boy was running away," which has a propositional object, entails "Jones saw a boy," which has only a noun object. More generally, whenever we can say, "S perceives that x is f" or "S perceives x to be f," we can infer "S perceives x" and "S perceives an f." But the converse does not hold. Given "S perceives an f," we cannot infer that there is an x such that S perceives that x is f. If, unknown to Jones, the boy he saw happened to be the thief who took the money, then we could say, "Jones saw a thief," even though Jones did not *take* him to be a thief. We could also say, "Jones saw the boy who took the money"—where the propositional clause, "who took the money," is not itself the object of the verb, but is a phrase modifying the nonpropositional object of the verb. We could *not* say, however, "Jones saw that the boy was the thief" or "Jones saw that the boy was the one who took the money." Once the thief is caught, Jones may then

---

[24] Usually when logicians talk about demonstrative or indexical terms, they do not allow for the possibility of "mistaken indication"—that is, the possibility that these terms may "purport to indicate" without indicating anything. But see Arthur W. Burks, "Icon, Index, and Symbol," *Philosophy and Phenomenological Research*, IX (1949), especially 688–689, and A. J. Ayer, *Philosophical Essays*, p. 80n. The phrase "purport to designate" is used by W. V. Quine; see *Methods of Logic* (New York, 1950), sec. 34.

say regretfully, "I saw the thief as he was making his getaway; it's a pity I didn't realize it at the time."

We have already noted that the propositional locution "S perceives *x* to be *f*" entails "S assumes—or accepts the proposition—that *x* is *f*." If Jones *saw that* the boy was running away, then, clearly, Jones accepted the proposition that the boy was running away. But the nonpropositional use of these words does not entail any such statements about accepting or assuming. One may say, quite consistently, "Jones saw the thief, but thought he was someone else and not the thief at all." [25] (I suggested, in Section 3 above, that a nonpropositional locution such as "Jones saw a thief," in its ordinary interpretation, may imply that Jones took—and thus believed—the thing he saw to be *something* or other. But it doesn't imply that he took it to be a thief.)

Occasionally our formulation of perceptual statements is ambiguous in that we do not make clear whether or not the object of the verb is to be taken propositionally. "Jones saw the thief running away" might mean, as in our present example, that the boy whom Jones saw was, unknown to Jones, a thief who was running away. But it might also mean the same as "Jones saw that the boy was a thief and that he was running away." And the denials of nonpropositional perceptual statements are sometimes ambiguous. We may say of a lady, trying to find a spoon on her kitchen shelf, "She was looking at it all the time and didn't see it!" But if she was looking at the spoon, she *did* see it; what she didn't see was that the thing she was looking at was the thing she was trying to find.

---

[25] Some of these points are also discussed in G. J. Warnock, "Seeing," *Proceedings of the Aristotelian Society* (vol. LV, 1954–1955), and G. N. A. Vesey, "Seeing and Seeing as," *Proceedings of the Aristotelian Society* (vol. LVI, 1955–1956). I have avoided "seeing as," in the present context, because this expression has a number of quite different uses in psychological literature.

Use of the first person introduces a further complication. Although one can say, "Jones sees a thief without realizing it," one cannot say, "I see a thief without realizing it." "I see a thief"—a first-person statement in the present tense—entails, or presupposes, "I take something to be a thief" or "I believe something to be a thief." [26] But "I *saw* a thief"—a first-person statement in the past tense—does *not* entail, or presuppose, that I believed or took anything to be a thief. And "I shall see a thief" may be used without implying that I shall believe the thing I see to be a thief.

Such verbs as "watch," "look at," "listen," "sniff," "savor," and "scrutinize" are closely related to our perception words. But unlike "see," "hear," and "perceive," they are ordinarily used to designate purposive *activities*. We can consent or refuse to watch, look, and listen; but we cannot—in the same sense —consent or refuse to see, hear, and perceive. We may watch or listen to something *carefully*, or *efficiently*, or *confidently*. But we cannot be said to see it, or to hear or perceive it, carefully, efficiently, or confidently.[27] These activity verbs—"watch," "listen," "look at," and the like—are nonpropositional; unlike "perceive" and "see," they do not take propositional clauses as their grammatical objects. But when we wish to describe the *successes* or *failures* of these activities, we must use perceptual words in their *propositional* senses. For these successes and failures are epistemic—and can be described only by means of

---

[26] Whether we use "entail" or some other word in this context depends on our solution to the puzzle: "If Thomas were honestly to assert, 'Mushrooms are poisonous, but I don't believe it,' would he be contradicting himself?" Max Black defines a relation of *presupposition* which he would substitute for that of *entailment* in such contexts; see his *Problems of Analysis*, ch. ii.

[27] See Ryle, *op. cit.*, pp. 149 ff., 238 ff. There is an excellent account of such words by F. N. Sibley in "Seeking, Scrutinizing, and Seeing," *Mind*, XLIV (1955), 455–478. See also Gwynneth Matthews, "A Note on Inference as Action," *Analysis*, XVI (1955), 116–117.

The Perception of Things

an epistemic vocabulary. If a man is watching, listening, examining, or investigating, then he has a purpose which can be fulfilled only if he perceives *that* a certain thing has a certain property.[28]

---

[28] I regret that I did not see J. R. Smythies' *Analysis of Perception* (London, 1956), until the present book was ready for publication. Smythies interprets the findings of contemporary neurology and neurophysiology and relates them to the philosophy of perception. Although I believe his interpretation presupposes solutions to some of the problems discussed here, much of what he says is relevant to what I have tried to say. Had I seen his book earlier, I would have expressed parts of the present chapter somewhat differently.

Eleven

"Intentional Inexistence"

1. I have suggested that the locution "There is something that S *perceives* to be *f*" may be defined as meaning: there is something such that it is *f*, it appears to S in some way, S takes it to be *f*, and S has adequate evidence for so doing. And I have suggested that "S *takes* something to be *f*" may be defined by reference to what S assumes, or accepts. I have now said all that I can about the philosophic questions which the concepts of *adequate evidence* and of *appearing* involve. Let us finally turn, then, to the concept of *assuming*, or *accepting*. The principal philosophic questions which this concept involves may be formulated by reference to a thesis proposed by Franz Brentano.

Psychological phenomena, according to Brentano, are characterized "by what the scholastics of the Middle Ages referred to as the intentional (also the mental) inexistence of the object, and what we, although with not quite unambiguous expressions, would call relation to a content, direction upon an object (which is not here to be understood as a reality), or immanent objectivity." [1] This "intentional inexistence," Brentano added, is peculiar to what is psychical; things which are merely physical show nothing like it.

Assuming, or *accepting*, is one of the phenomena Brentano would have called intentional. I will first try to formulate Brentano's thesis somewhat more exactly; then I will ask whether it is true of assuming.

2. The phenomena most clearly illustrating the concept of "intentional inexistence" are what are sometimes called psychological attitudes; for example, desiring, hoping, wishing, seeking, believing, and assuming. When Brentano said that these attitudes "intentionally contain an object in themselves," he was referring to the fact that they can be truly said to "have objects" even though the objects which they can be said to have do not in fact exist. Diogenes could have looked for an honest man even if there hadn't been any honest men. The horse can desire to be fed even though he won't be fed. James could believe there are tigers in India, and *take* something there to be a tiger, even if there aren't any tigers in India.

But *physical*—or nonpsychological—phenomena, according to Brentano's thesis, cannot thus "intentionally contain objects in themselves." In order for Diogenes to sit in his tub, for example, there must be a tub for him to sit in; in order for the horse to eat his oats, there must be oats for him to eat; and in order for James to shoot a tiger, there must be a tiger there to shoot.

The statements used in these examples seem to have the form of relational statements. "Diogenes sits in his tub" is concerned with a relation between Diogenes and his tub. Syntactically, at least, "Diogenes looks for an honest man" is simi-

---

[1] Franz Brentano, *Psychologie vom empirischen Standpunkte* (Leipzig, 1924), I, 124–125.

lar: Diogenes' quest seems to relate him in a certain way to honest men. But the relations described in this and in our other psychological statements, if they can properly be called "relations," are of a peculiar sort. They can hold even though one of their terms, if it can properly be called a "term," does not exist. It may seem, therefore, that one can be "intentionally related" to something which does not exist.[2]

These points can be put somewhat more precisely by referring to the language we have used. We may say that, in our language, the expressions "looks for," "expects," and "believes" occur in sentences which are intentional, or are used intentionally, whereas "sits in," "eats," and "shoots" do not. We can formulate a working criterion by means of which we can distinguish sentences that are intentional, or are used intentionally, in a certain language from sentences that are not. It is easy to see, I think, what this criterion would be like, if stated for ordinary English.

First, let us say that a simple declarative sentence is intentional if it uses a substantival expression—a name or a description—in such a way that neither the sentence nor its contradictory implies either that there is or that there isn't anything to which the substantival expression truly applies. "Diogenes looked for an honest man" is intentional by this criterion. Neither "Diogenes looked for an honest man" nor its contradictory—"Diogenes did *not* look for an honest man"—implies either that there are, or that there are not, any honest men. But "Diogenes sits in his tub" is not intentional by this criterion, for it implies that there *is* a tub in which he sits.

Secondly, let us say, of any noncompound sentence which

---

[2] But the point of talking about "intentionality" is not that there is a peculiar type of "inexistent" object; it is rather that there is a type of psychological phenomenon which is unlike anything purely physical. In his later writings Brentano explicitly rejected the view that there are "inexistent objects"; see his *Psychologie*, II, 133 ff., and *Wahrheit und Evidenz* (Leipzig, 1930), pp. 87, 89.

contains a propositional clause, that it is intentional provided that neither the sentence nor its contradictory implies either that the propositional clause is true or that it is false. "James believes there are tigers in India" is intentional by this criterion, because neither it nor its contradictory implies either that there are, or that there are not, any tigers in India. "He succeeded in visiting India," since it implies that he did visit India, is not intentional. "He is able to visit India," although it does not imply that he will visit India, is also not intentional. For its contradictory—"He is not able to visit India"—implies that he does *not* visit India.

A third mark of intentionality may be described in this way. Suppose there are two names or descriptions which designate the same things and that *E* is a sentence obtained merely by separating these two names or descriptions by means of "is identical with" (or "are identical with" if the first word is plural). Suppose also that *A* is a sentence using one of those names or descriptions and that *B* is like *A* except that, where *A* uses the one, *B* uses the other. Let us say that *A* is intentional if the conjunction of *A* and *E* does not imply *B*.³ We can now say of certain cognitive sentences—sentences using "know," "see," "perceive," and the like in one of the ways which have interested us here—that they, too, are intentional. Most of us knew in 1944 that Eisenhower was the one in command (*A*); but although he was (identical with) the man who was to succeed Truman (*E*), it is not true that we knew in 1944 that the man who was to succeed Truman was the one in command (*B*).

Let us say that a *compound* sentence is one compounded

---

³ This third mark is essentially the same as Frege's concept of "indirect reference." See Gottlob Frege, "Über Sinn und Bedeutung," *Zeitschrift für Philosophie und philosophische Kritik*, n.s. C (1892), 25–50, especially 38; reprinted in Herbert Feigl and W. S. Sellars, eds., *Readings in Philosophical Analysis* (New York, 1949), and Peter Geach and Max Black, eds., *Philosophical Writings of Gottlob Frege* (Oxford, 1952).

from two or more sentences by means of propositional con-
nectives, such as "and," "or," "if-then," "although," "because,"
and the like. The three foregoing marks of intentionality apply
to sentences which are *not* compound. We may now say that
a compound declarative sentence is intentional if and only if
one or more of its component sentences is intentional. Thus
the antecedent of "If Parsifal sought the Holy Grail, he was a
Christian" enables us to say that the whole statement is intentional.

When we use perception words propositionally, our sentences display the third of the above marks of intentionality. I
may see that John is the man in the corner and John may be
someone who is ill; but I do not now *see* that John is someone
who is ill. Perception sentences, as we have seen, entail sentences about taking and assuming. And sentences about taking
and assuming display the second of the above marks of intentionality. "He takes—and therefore assumes—those rocks
to be the reef" does not imply that the rocks *are* the reef and
it does not imply that they are not. And similarly for its contradiction: "He does not take—or assume—those rocks to be
the reef."

We may now re-express Brentano's thesis—or a thesis re-
sembling that of Brentano—by reference to intentional sentences. Let us say (1) that we do not need to use intentional
sentences when we describe nonpsychological phenomena; we
can express all of our beliefs about what is merely "physical"
in sentences which are not intentional.[4] But (2) when we
wish to describe perceiving, assuming, believing, knowing, want-

---

[4] There are sentences describing relations of comparison—for example,
"Some lizards look like dragons"—which may constitute an exception to
(1). If they are exceptions, then we may qualify (1) to read: "We do not
need any intentional sentences, other than those describing relations of comparison, when we describe nonpsychological phenomena." This qualification
would not affect any of the points to be made here.

172

ing, hoping, and other such attitudes, then either (a) we must use sentences which are intentional or (b) we must use terms we do not need to use when we describe nonpsychological phenomena.

In describing nonpsychological phenomena, we do, on occasion, use sentences which are intentional by one or more of the above criteria. One may say, "This weapon, suitably placed, is capable of causing the destruction of Boston" and "The cash register knows that 7 and 5 are 12." But although these sentences are intentional according to our criteria, we can readily transform them into others which are not: "If this weapon were suitably placed, then Boston would be destroyed" and "If you press the key marked '7' and the one marked '5', the cash register will yield a slip marked '12.'"

It would be an easy matter, of course, to invent a psychological terminology enabling us to describe perceiving, taking, and assuming in sentences which are not intentional. Instead of saying, for example, that a man *takes* something to be a deer, we could say "His perceptual environment is deer-inclusive." But in so doing, we are using technical terms—"perceptual environment" and "deer-inclusive"—which, presumably, are not needed for the description of nonpsychological phenomena. And unless we can re-express the deer-sentence once again, this time as a nonintentional sentence containing no such technical terms, what we say about the man and the deer will conform to our present version of Brentano's thesis.

How would we go about showing that Brentano was wrong? I shall consider the three most likely methods. None of them seems to be satisfactory.

3. Some philosophers have tried to describe psychological attitudes in terms of *linguistic* behavior. In his inaugural lecture, *Thinking and Meaning*, Professor Ayer tried to define the

locution "thinking of *x*" by reference to the use of symbols which designate *x*. A man is *thinking of* a unicorn, Ayer suggested, if (among other things) the man is disposed to use symbols which *designate* unicorns; he *believes* that there are unicorns if (among other things) he is disposed to utter sentences containing words which *designate* or *refer to* unicorns.[5] And perhaps one might try to define "taking" and "assuming" in a similar way. But this type of definition leaves us with our problem.

When we talk about what is "designated" or "referred to" by words or sentences, our own sentences are intentional. When we affirm the sentence "In German, *Einhorn* designates, or refers to, unicorns," we do not imply that there are any unicorns and we do not imply that there are not; and similarly when we deny the sentence. If we think of words and sentences as classes of noises and marks, then we may say that words and sentences are "physical" (nonpsychological) phenomena. But we must not suppose the meaning of words and sentences to be a property which they have apart from their relations to the psychological attitudes of the people who *use* them.

For we know, as Schlick once put it, "that meaning does not inhere in a sentence where it might be discovered"; meaning "must be bestowed upon" the sentence.[6] Instead of say-

---

[5] A. J. Ayer, *Thinking and Meaning*, p. 13. Compare W. S. Sellars, "Mind, Meaning, and Behavior," *Philosophical Studies*, III (1952) 83–95; "A Semantical Solution of the Mind-Body Problem," *Methodos* (1953), pp. 45–85; and "Empiricism and the Philosophy of Mind," in Herbert Feigl and Michael Scriven, eds., *The Foundations of Science and the Concepts of Psychology and Psychoanalysis* (Minneapolis, 1956). See also Leonard Bloomfield, *Linguistic Aspects of Science* (Chicago, 1939), pp. 17–19.

[6] Moritz Schlick, "Meaning and Verification," *Philosophical Review*, XLV (1936), 348; reprinted in Feigl and Sellars, eds., *Readings in Philosophical Analysis*. Compare this analogy, in "Meaning and Free Will," by John Hospers: "Sentences in themselves do not possess meaning; it is mis-

ing, "In German, *Einhorn* designates, or refers to, unicorns," we could say, less misleadingly, "German-speaking people use the word *Einhorn* in order to designate, or refer to, unicorns." A word or sentence designates so-and-so only if people *use* it to designate so-and-so.

Or can we describe "linguistic behavior" by means of sentences which are not intentional? Can we define such locutions as "the word '*Q*' designates so-and-so" in language which is not intentional? If we can do these things, and if, as Ayer suggested, we can define "believing," or "assuming," in terms of linguistic behavior, then we must reject our version of Brentano's thesis. But I do not believe that we can do these things; I do not believe that we can define such locutions as "The word '*Q*' designates so-and-so" or "The word '*Q*' has such-and-such a *use*" in language which is not intentional.

Let us consider, briefly, the difficulties involved in one attempt to formulate such a definition.

Instead of saying, of a certain word or predicate "*Q*," that it designates or refers to so-and-so's, we may say that, if there were any so-and-so's, they would satisfy or fulfill the *intension* of the predicate "*Q*." But how are we to define "intension"? Professor Carnap once proposed a behavioristic definition of this use of "intension" which, if it were adequate, might enable us to formulate a behavioristic, nonintentional definition of "believe" and "assume." Although Carnap later conceded that his account was oversimplified, it is instructive, I think, to note the difficulties which stand in the way of

---

leading to speak of 'the meaning of sentences' at all; meaning being conferred in every case by the speaker, the sentence's meaning is only like the light of the moon: without the sun to give it light, it would possess none. And for an analysis of the light we must go to the sun" (*Philosophy and Phenomenological Research*, X [1950], 308).

Perceiving

defining "intension"—as well as "designates" and "refers to"—in nonintentional terms.[7]

Carnap had suggested that the "intension" of a predicate in a natural language may be defined in essentially this way: "The intension of a predicate 'Q' for a speaker X is the general condition which an object y must fulfill in order for X to be willing to ascribe the predicate 'Q' to y." Carnap did not define the term "ascribe" which appears in this definition, but from his general discussion we can see, I think, that he would have said something very much like this: "A person X ascribes 'Q' to an object y, provided that, in the presence of y, X gives an affirmative response to the question 'Q?'" (Let us assume that the expressions "is willing to," "in the presence of," "affirmative response," and "question" present no difficulties.)

Such a definition of "intension" is adequate only if it allows us to say of Karl, who speaks German, that an object y fulfills the intension of "Hund" for Karl if and only if y is a dog. Let us consider, then, a situation in which Karl mistakes something for a dog; he is in the presence of a fox, say, and takes it to be a dog. In this case, Karl would be willing to give an affirmative response to the question "Hund?" Hence the fox fulfills the condition which an object must fulfill for Karl to be willing to ascribe "Hund" to it. And therefore the definition is inadequate.

Perhaps we can assume that Karl is usually right when he takes something to be a dog. And perhaps, therefore, we can say this: "The intension of 'Hund' for Karl is the general condition which, more often than not, an object y must fulfill in

---

[7] Carnap's definition appeared on p. 42 of "Meaning and Synonymy in Natural Languages," *Philosophical Studies*, IV (1955), 33–47. In "On Some Concepts of Pragmatics," *Philosophical Studies*, VI, 89–91, he conceded that "designates" should be defined in terms of "believes." The second article was written in reply to my "A Note on Carnap's Meaning Analysis," which appeared in the same issue (pp. 87–89).

176

order for Karl to be willing to ascribe '*Hund*' to *y*." But if the occasion we have considered is the only one on which Karl has been in the presence of a *fox*, then, according to the present suggestion, we must say, falsely, that the fox does not fulfill the intension of Karl's word *"Fuchs."* Moreover, if Karl believes there are unicorns and, on the sole occasion when he thinks he sees one, mistakes a horse for a unicorn, then the present suggestion would require us to say, falsely, that the horse fulfills the intension, for Karl, of his word *"Einhorn."*

The obvious way to qualify Carnap's definition would be to reintroduce the term "believe" and say something of this sort: "The intension of a predicate '*Q*' for a speaker X is the general condition which X must *believe* an object *y* to fulfill in order for X to be willing to ascribe the predicate '*Q*' to *y*." And, in general, when we say, "People use such and such a word to refer to so-and-so," at least part of what we mean to say is that people use that word when they wish to express or convey something they *know* or *believe*—or *perceive* or *take* —with respect to so-and-so. But if we define "intension" and "designates" in terms of "believe" and "assume," we can no longer hope, of course, to define "believe" and "assume" in terms of "intension" or "designates."

4. The second way in which we might try to show that Brentano was wrong may be described by reference to a familiar conception of "sign behavior." Many philosophers and psychologists have suggested, in effect, that a man may be said to *perceive* an object *x*, or to *take* some object *x* to have a certain property *f*, provided only that there is something which *signifies* *x* to him, or which signifies to him that *x* is *f*. But what does "signify" mean?

We cannot be satisfied with the traditional descriptions of "sign behavior," for these, almost invariably, define such terms as "sign" by means of intentional concepts. We cannot say, for instance, that an object is a sign provided it causes someone to *believe*, or *expect*, or *think of* something; for sentences using "believe," "expect," and "think of" are clearly intentional. Nor can we say merely that an object is a sign provided it causes someone to be *set for*, or to be *ready for*, or to *behave appropriately to* something, for sentences using "set for," "ready for," and "behave appropriately to," despite their behavioristic overtones, are also intentional. Similar objections apply to such statements as "One object is a sign of another provided it *introduces* the other object *into the behaviorial environment*, as contrasted with the physical environment, of some organism."

If we are to show that Brentano's thesis as applied to *sign* phenomena is mistaken, then we must not introduce any new technical terms into our analysis of sign behavior unless we can show that these terms apply also to nonpsychological situations.

Most attempts at nonintentional definitions of "sign" make use of the concept of *substitute stimulus*. If we use "referent" as short for "what is signified," we may say that, according to such definitions, the sign is described as a substitute for the referent. It is a substitute in the sense that, as stimulus, it has effects upon the subject which are similar to those the referent would have had. Such definitions usually take this form: V is a *sign* of R for a subject S if and only if V affects S in a manner similar to that in which R would have affected S.[8] The bell is

---

[8] Compare Charles E. Osgood, *Method and Theory in Experimental Psychology* (New York, 1953), p. 696: "A pattern of stimulation which is not the object is a sign of the object if it evokes in an organism a mediating reaction, this (a) being some fractional part of the total behavior elicited by the object and (b) producing distinctive self-stimulation that mediates responses which would not occur without the previous association of non-object and object patterns of stimulation. All of these limiting conditions seem necessary. The mediation process must include part of the same be-

a sign of food to the dog, because the bell affects the dog's responses, or his dispositions to respond, in a way similar to that in which the food would have affected them.

This type of definition involves numerous difficulties of which we need mention but one—that of specifying the respect or degree of similarity which must obtain between the effects attributed to the sign and those attributed to the referent. This difficulty is involved in every version of the substitute-stimulus theory. Shall we say that, given the conditions in the above definition, V is a sign of R to a subject S provided only that those responses of S which are stimulated by V are similar in *some* respect to those which have been (or would be) stimulated by R? In other words, should we say that V is a sign of R provided that V has some of the effects which R has had or would have had? This would have the unacceptable consequence that all stimuli signify each other, since any two stimuli have at least some effect in common. Every stimulus causes neural activity, for example; hence, to that extent at least, any two stimuli will have similar effects. Shall we say that V is a sign of R provided that V has *all* the effects which R would have had? If the bell is to have all the effects which the food would have had, then, as Morris notes, the dog must start to eat the bell.[9] Shall we say that V is a sign of R provided that V has the effects which *only* R would have had? If the sign has

---

havior made to the object if the sign is to have its representing property." Some of the difficulties of the substitute stimulus concept [qualification (a) in this definition] are met by qualification (b), which implies that the subject must once have perceived the thing signified. But (b) introduces new difficulties. Since I have never seen the President of the United States, no announcement, according to this definition, could signify to me that the President is about to arrive.

[9] See Charles Morris, *Signs, Language, and Behavior*, p. 12, and Max Black, "The Limitations of a Behavioristic Semiotic," *Philosophical Review*, LVI (1947), 258–272.

effects which only the referent can have, then the sign *is* the referent and only food can be a sign of food. The other methods of specifying the degree or respect of similarity required by the substitute-stimulus definition, so far as I can see, have equally unacceptable consequences.

Reichenbach, in his *Elements of Symbolic Logic*, has applied this type of analysis to the concept of taking; but the consequences are similar. To say of a subject S, according to Reichenbach, that S *takes* something to be a dog is to say: "There is a z which is a bodily state of S and which is such that, whenever S is sensibly stimulated by a dog, S is in this bodily state z." [10] In other words, there are certain bodily conditions which S must fulfill in order for S to be sensibly stimulated by a dog; and whenever S satisfies any of these conditions, then S is taking something to be a dog.

But among the many conditions one must fulfill if one is to be sensibly stimulated by a dog is that of being alive. Hence if we know that S is alive, we can say that S is taking something to be a dog. The difficulty is that the bodily state z, of Reichenbach's formula, is not specified strictly enough. And the problem is to find an acceptable modification.

In reply to this objection, Reichenbach suggested, in effect, that "S takes something to be a dog" means that S's bodily state has all those neural properties which it must have— which are "physically necessary" for it to have—whenever S is sensibly stimulated by a dog.[11] But this definition has the

---

[10] This is a paraphrase of what Hans Reichenbach formulated in special symbols on p. 275 of *Elements of Symbolic Logic* (New York, 1947).

[11] Reichenbach suggests this motification in "On Observing and Perceiving," *Philosophical Studies*, II (1951), pp. 92–93. This paper was written in reply to my "Reichenbach on Observing and Perceiving" (*Philosophical Studies*, II, 45–48), which contains some of the above criticisms. In these papers, as well as in Reichenbach's original discussion, the word "perceive" was used in the way in which we have been using "take." Reichenbach used

unacceptable consequence that, whenever S is sensibly stimulated by a dog, then S *takes* the thing to be a dog. Thus,
although we can say that a man may be stimulated by a fox
and yet take it to be a dog, we can never say that he may be
stimulated by a dog and *not* take it to be a dog.[12]

Similar objections apply to definitions using such expressions
as "dog responses," "responses specific to dogs," "responses
appropriate to dogs," and the like. For the problem of specifying what a man's "dog responses" might be is essentially that
of specifying the bodily state to which Reichenbach referred.

5. Of all intentional phenomena, expectation is one of the
most simple and, I think, one which is most likely to be definable in terms which are not intentional. If we could define,
in nonintentional terms, what it means to say of a man, or an
animal, that he expects something—that he expects some state
of affairs to come about—then, perhaps, we could define "believing" and "assuming," nonintentionally, in terms of this
sense of "expecting." If we are to show that Brentano is wrong,
our hope lies here, I think.

For every expectancy, there is some possible state of affairs
which would *fulfill* or *satisfy* it, and another possible state of
affairs which would *frustrate* or *disrupt* it. If I expect the car

the term "immediate existence" in place of Brentano's "intentional inexistence"; see *Elements of Symbolic Logic*, p. 274.

[12] This sort of modification may suggest itself: Consider those bodily states
which are such that (i) S is in those states whenever he is sensibly stimulated by a dog and (ii) S cannot be in those states whenever he is *not* being
stimulated by a dog. Shall we say "S takes something to be a dog" means
that S is in this particular class of states? If we define "taking" in this way,
then, we must say that, in the present state of psychology and physiology,
we have no way of knowing whether anyone ever *does* take anything to be
a dog, much less whether people take things to be dogs on just those occasions on which we want to be able to *say* that they take things to be dogs.

to stop, then, it would seem, I am in a state which would be fulfilled or satisfied if and only if the car were to stop—and which would be frustrated or disrupted if and only if the car were not to stop. Hence we might consider defining "expects" in this way:

> "S *expects* E to occur" means that S is in a bodily state *b* such that either (i) *b* would be fulfilled if and only if E were to occur or (ii) *b* would be disrupted if and only if E were not to occur.

Our problem now becomes that of finding appropriate meanings for "fulfill" and "disrupt."

Perhaps there is a way of defining "fulfill" in terms of the psychological concept of *re-enforcement* and of defining "disrupt" in terms of *disequilibration, surprise,* or *shock.* And perhaps we can then provide an account of the dog and the bell and the food in terms which will show that this elementary situation is not intentional. It is possible that the dog, because of the sound of the bell, is in a state which is such that either (i) his state will be re-enforced if he receives food or (ii) it will be disequilibrated if he does not. And it is possible that this state can be specified in physiological terms. Whether this is so, of course, is a psychological question which no one, apparently, is yet in a position to answer. But even if it is so, there are difficulties in principle which appear when we try to apply this type of definition to human behavior.

If we apply "expects," as defined, to human behavior, then we must say that the appropriate fulfillments or disruptions must be caused by the occurrence, or nonoccurrence, of the "intentional object"—of *what* it is that is expected. But it is easy to think of situations which, antecedently, we should want to describe as instances of expectation, but in which the fulfillments or disruptions do not occur in the manner required. And to accommodate our definition to such cases, we must make qualifications which can be expressed only by reintroducing the intentional concepts we are trying to eliminate.

This difficulty may be illustrated as follows: Jones, let us suppose, *expects* to meet his aunt at the railroad station within twenty-five minutes. Our formulation, as applied to this situation, would yield: "Jones is in a bodily state which would be fulfilled if he were to meet his aunt at the station within twenty-five minutes or which would be disrupted if he were not to meet her there within that time." But what if he were to meet his aunt and yet *take* her to be someone else? Or if he were to meet someone else and yet *take* her to be his aunt? In such cases, the fulfillments and disruptions would not occur in the manner required by our definition.

If we introduce the intentional term "perceives" or "takes" into our definition of "expects," in order to say, in this instance, that Jones *perceives* his aunt, or *takes* someone to be his aunt, then, of course, we can no longer define "assume"—or "perceive" and "take"—in terms of "expects." It is worth noting, moreover, that even if we allow ourselves the intentional term "perceive" our definition will be inadequate. Suppose that Jones were to visit the bus terminal, believing it to be the railroad station, or that he were to visit the railroad station believing it to be the bus terminal. If he met his aunt at the railroad station, believing it to be the bus terminal, then, contrary to our formula, he may be frustrated or surprised, and, if he fails to meet her there, his state may be fulfilled. Hence we must add further qualifications about what he believes or doesn't believe.[13]

---

[13] R. B. Braithwaite in "Belief and Action" (*Aristotelian Society*, suppl. vol. XX [1946] p. 10) suggests that a man may be said to believe a proposition *p* provided this condition obtains: "If at a time when an occasion arises relevant to *p*, his springs of action are *s*, he will perform an action which

Perceiving

If his visit to the station is brief and if he is not concerned about his aunt, the requisite re-enforcement or frustration may still fail to occur. Shall we add ". . . provided he *looks for* his aunt"? But now we have an intentional expression again. And even if we allow him to look for her, the re-enforcement or frustration may fail to occur if he finds himself able to satisfy desires which are more compelling than that of finding his aunt.

We seem to be led back, then, to the intentional language with which we began. In attempting to apply our definition of "expects" to a situation in which "expects" is ordinarily applicable, we find that we must make certain qualifications and that these qualifications can be formulated only by using intentional terms. We have had to introduce qualifications wherein we speak of the subject *perceiving* or *taking* something to be the object expected; hence we cannot now define "perceive" and "assume" in terms of "expect." We have had to add that the subject has certain *beliefs* concerning the nature of the conditions under which he perceives, or fails to perceive, the ob-

---

is such that, if p is true, it will tend to fulfill s, and which is such that, if p is false, it will not tend to satisfy s." But the definition needs qualifications in order to exclude those people who, believing truly (p) that the water is deep at the base of Niagara Falls and wishing (s) to survive a trip over the falls, have yet acted in a way which has not tended to satisfy s. Moreover, if we are to use such a definition to show that Brentano was wrong, we must provide a nonintentional definition of the present use of "wish" or "spring of action." And, with Braithwaite's definition of "believe," it would be difficult to preserve the distinction which, apparently, we ought to make between *believing* a proposition and *acting upon* it (see Chapter One, Section 2). I have proposed detailed criticisms of a number of such definitions of "believe" in "Sentences about Believing," *Proceedings of the Aristotelian Society*, LVI (1955–1956), 125–148. Some of the difficulties involved in defining *purpose* nonintentionally are pointed out by Richard Taylor in "Comments on a Mechanistic Conception of Purpose," *Philosophy of Science*, XVII (1950), 310–317, and "Purposeful and Nonpurposeful Behavior: A Rejoinder," *ibid.*, 327–332.

ject. And we have referred to what he is *looking for* and to his other possible *desires*.

It may be that some of the simple "expectancies" we attribute to infants or to animals can be described, nonintentionally, in terms of re-enforcement or frustration. And possibly, as Ogden and Richards intimated, someone may yet find a way of show-ing that believing, perceiving, and taking are somehow "theoret-ically analysable" into such expectancies.[14] But until such programs are carried out, there is, I believe, some justification for saying that Brentano's thesis does apply to the concept of *perceiving.*

---

[14] C. K. Ogden and I. A. Richards, *The Meaning of Meaning,* 5th ed. (London, 1938), p. 71.

Appendix and Index

Appendix

Phenomenalism

1. Ernst Mach expressed *phenomenalism* by saying that "all bodies are but thought-symbols for complexes of sensations." [1] Where Mach uses "sensations" other phenomenalists may use "appearances" or "sense-data." And where Mach uses "thought-symbols," others may talk about language and "rules of translation." [2] But every form of phenomenalism involves the thesis that anything we know about material things may be expressed in statements referring solely to appearances. Since many of the problems I have discussed in this book would require a very different treatment if this thesis were true, I shall now state my reasons for believing it to be false.

---

[1] Ernst Mach, *The Analysis of Sensations* (Chicago, 1897), p. 22.

[2] Compare A. J. Ayer, *The Foundations of Empirical Knowledge:* "What is being claimed is simply that the propositions which are ordinarily expressed by sentences which refer to material things could also be expressed by sentences which referred exclusively to sense-data" (p. 232). C. I. Lewis has noted that the label "phenomenalism" is not altogether appropriate for the view here in question; see "Realism or Phenomenalism?" *Philosophical Review*, LXIV (1955), 233–247.

Appendix

2. I have said that whenever we perceive anything x to have some property f we have certain beliefs about the ways in which x appears. If a man now takes something to be a tree, he believes that, under the conditions now obtaining, he would *not* be appeared to in just the way he is appeared to unless the thing were a tree. And he believes that if he were now to act in certain ways—if he were to approach the thing he takes to be a tree, or if he were to reach out and touch it—he would be appeared to in still other ways characteristic of a tree. It is accurate to say, I think, that phenomenalism is based upon an interpretation of such facts as these.

The phenomenalist contends that, if we ask ourselves just what it is we are believing when we think we perceive something to have a certain characteristic, we will find that our beliefs really pertain only to the *appearances* of the thing we think we are perceiving. He then infers that our ordinary statements about physical things—such statements as "That is a tree" and "This thing is red"—logically *entail* many statements referring solely to appearances. And he concludes that, if only we were to list the appearance statements entailed by any thing statement, we would have for that thing statement the type of translation the phenomenalistic thesis requires: we would have a set of appearance statements expressing everything that the thing statement is ordinarily used to express.

But is it true that such statements as "That is a tree" and "This thing is red" *entail* any statements referring solely to appearances—to ways of sensing? The familiar facts of "perceptual relativity" suggest that our ordinary thing statements do *not* entail any statements referring solely to appearances.[3]

Whether a material thing will ever present, say, a red appearance depends partly upon the nature of the thing and

---

[3] We should say, more exactly, that such thing statements entail no *synthetic*, or *nonlogical*, statements referring solely to appearances.

partly upon the conditions under which the thing is perceived. If one knew that the thing was red and that the lighting conditions were normal, one could predict that, to a normal observer, the thing would present a red appearance; if one knew that the lights were out, or that the perceiver had a certain kind of color blindness, one could predict that the thing would present some other appearance; and so on, for any other thing and its possible appearances. To calculate the appearances, it is necessary to know both the thing perceived and the observation conditions, for it is the thing perceived and the observation conditions working jointly which determine the way the thing is to appear.

The facts of perceptual relativity thus suggest that even the simple thing statement, "This thing is red," doesn't entail *any* statement about appearances; an appearance statement is entailed only when "This thing is red" is taken in conjunction with *another* thing statement referring to observation conditions. This may be seen further if we compare first the thing statement

This is red (P)

and a categorical appearance statement

Redness will be sensed. (R)

(In his use of such words as "appearance" and "sense," the phenomenalist may allow himself more freedom than would be condoned by the view about appearing advocated in Chapter Eight. But I shall not presuppose this view in what follows.)

May we say, then, that the statement P above entails R, as these statements would ordinarily be interpreted? Possibly it is obvious that no contradiction is involved in affirming P and denying R. The following considerations, however, may make the matter clearer.

Appendix

Taken in conjunction with certain *other* thing statements Q, referring to observation conditions, P does entail R. The following is such a statement Q:

This is perceived under normal conditions; and if this is red and is perceived under normal conditions, redness will be sensed. (Q)

(So far as our present point is concerned, it does not particularly matter how the expression "normal conditions" is defined.)

Taken in conjunction, not with Q, but with still *other* thing statements S, also referring to observation conditions, P entails not-R. An example of S would be:

This is perceived under conditions which are normal except for the presence of blue lights; and if this is red and is perceived under conditions which are normal except for the presence of blue lights, redness will not be sensed. (S)

As these statements would ordinarily be interpreted, S is logically consistent with P; there is no contradiction involved in affirming one and denying the other. But the conjunction of P and S, if it is logically consistent, must entail everything that P entails and cannot entail anything logically incompatible with what P entails. If P and S entail not-R, it is impossible that P entail R. Hence "This is red" (P) does not entail "Redness will be sensed" (R). Similarly, "Redness will not be sensed" is not sufficient to *falsify* "This is red." We may draw a similar conclusion with respect to any other categorical appearance statement R'. Although there may be a statement about observation conditions, Q', such that "This is red" (P) and Q' entail R', there is also a statement about observation conditions, S', such that P and S' entail not-R'; hence P does not entail R'.

According to some phenomenalists, the appearance statements entailed by statements describing a physical thing would be considerably more complicated than "Redness will be sensed"; they would be conjunctions of conditionals of the form "If such and such should be sensed, then such and such would be sensed." The phenomenalist might hold, for example, that the thing statement

There is really a door in front of me (*P*)

entails a conditional appearance statement of this sort:

If such-and-such visual appearances should be sensed (namely, those associated with reaching), then such-and-such tactual appearances would be sensed. (*R*)

Again, if *P* entails *R*, then it is logically impossible that there be a statement *S*, consistent with *P* and such that *P* and *S* entail not-*R*. Clearly there are many such statements *S*. If I am subject to systematic delusions, then one might be:

Whenever I see a door, I sense such-and-such visual appearances but not such-and-such tactual appearances.[4] (*S*)

This statement, in conjunction with *P*, entails not-*R*. Since *S* is consistent with *P*, it is false that *P* entails *R*.

By similar reasoning it would seem possible to formulate, for any complex appearance statement *R'* that might be thought to be an analytic consequence of *P*, some statement *S'* consistent with *P* and such that *P* and *S'* entail not-*R'*.

I believe we may say, therefore, that no synthetic thing

---

[4] Compare C. I. Lewis's example in *An Analysis of Knowledge and Valuation*, pp. 248–249, where appearance statements are said to be "probability consequences" of thing statements. Whether Lewis's view is an instance of phenomenalism depends upon how *probability* is interpreted; see George Chatalian, "Probability: Inductive versus Deductive," *Philosophical Studies*, III (1952), 49–56, and Roderick Firth, "Radical Empiricism and Perceptual Relativity," *Philosophical Review*, LIX (1950), 164–183, 319–331.

statement *P* entails any appearance statement unless *P* is taken in conjunction with some *other* thing statement referring to observation conditions. In our earlier example, "This is red" (*P*) does entail an appearance statement when *P* is conjoined with *Q*: "This is perceived under normal conditions; and if this is red and is perceived under normal conditions redness will be sensed." And we have seen that, when conjoined with statements about different observation conditions, "This is red" may entail a different statement about appearances. Thus when John Stuart Mill tried to show, with respect to his belief that Calcutta exists, that it can be expressed phenomenalistically, in terms of "permanent possibilities of sensations," he specified these possibilities by reference to himself and to the banks of the Hooghly:

I believe that Calcutta exists, though I do not perceive it, and that it would still exist if every percipient inhabitant were suddenly to leave the place, or be struck dead. But when I analyze the belief, all I find in it is, that were these events to take place, the Permanent Possibility of Sensation which I call Calcutta would still remain; that if I were suddenly transported to the banks of the Hooghly, I should still have the sensations which, if now present, would lead me to affirm that Calcutta exists here and now.[5]

But this method of deriving appearance statements from thing statements does not suggest any way of expressing "Calcutta

---

[5] John Stuart Mill, *An Examination of Sir William Hamilton's Philosophy* (New York, 1884), p. 246. Compare H. H. Price's criticism of such theories in *Hume's Theory of the External World* (Oxford, 1940), pp. 183–188. Roderick Firth has proposed a rather complex theory about the meaning of ordinary thing statements in order to deal with such problems (*op. cit.*, especially pp. 319–323). I cannot here do justice to his theory, but I believe it is fair to say: (i) the theory has some implausible consequences; (ii) it was designed with the purpose of adapting phenomenalism to considerations such as the above; and (iii) if the criticism of the ostensible *grounds* of phenomenalism, in Section 3 below, is accurate, then there is no positive reason for accepting Firth's theory.

exists" or "This thing is red" in terms referring solely to permanent possibilities of sensation, or to appearances. For we obtain our appearance statements only by referring to still other physical things.[6]

3. Why should one think that phenomenalism is true? If we look to the reasons phenomenalists have proposed, we will find, I think, that each is inconsistent with at least one of the conclusions of the present book. The most important of these reasons are the following three.[7]

(i) Professor Lewis has said that, if phenomenalism cannot be successfully defended, "then there will be nothing left for us but skepticism." [8] In saying this, he assumed, I think, that some form of *empiricism* (as defined in Chapter Six) is true. He assumed, first, with respect to those statements we would ordinarily justify by reference to perceiving, that no such statement is evident unless it is more probable than not in relation

---

[6] In *Berkeley* (pp. 183–189), G. J. Warnock compares the relation between thing statements and appearance statements to that between the *verdict* a jury makes and the *evidence* to which the jury appeals. But any verdict that is just and reasonable is probable—more probable than not—in relation to its evidence. And I have suggested in Chapter Six that there is no statement about a material thing which is more probable than not in relation to any set of statements referring merely to appearances.

[7] Phenomenalism has been defended by saying that, if statements about physical things have any *meaning* at all, they are translatable into statements about appearances. Little is gained by introducing the concept of *meaning* into the discussion, however, inasmuch as the positive grounds for this view of meaning are presumably the same as those for phenomenalism. And when phenomenalism is expressed this way, the phenomenalist's problem becomes that of showing that thing statements *do* have meaning, in this sense of "meaning"; for it would be misleading to use the word "meaning" in such a way that the statement "This thing is red" could *not* be said to mean anything.

[8] C. I. Lewis, "Professor Chisholm and Empiricism," *Journal of Philosophy*, XLV (1948), 519.

to statements about appearing. He assumed, secondly, that if we are thus confined to appearances and if phenomenalism is false then skepticism is true. And he assumed, thirdly, that if phenomenalism is true then, even though we may be so confined, skepticism is false. But according to the theory of evidence I attempted to defend in Chapter Six, there is no reason to accept the first of these assumptions. The statements we would ordinarily defend by reference to perceiving may be evident even though they are not probable in relation to statements about appearing. And therefore we need not accept the thesis that if phenomenalism cannot be successfully defended "there is nothing left for us but skepticism." [9]

(ii) I think that many philosophers have been led to accept phenomenalism because of what they believe about the genesis of our knowledge. They have assumed: first, that "before we can learn about the things that appear to us, we must learn about their appearances"; secondly, that the psychological process of perceiving developed from the more simple process of sensing appearances; and, thirdly, that this process could not have taken place unless phenomenalism is true. In Chapter Nine, Section 4, I discussed the first of these assumptions and suggested an alternative. If the suggested alternative is true, then, I think, there is no reason for supposing that the *second* of these assumptions is true. Moreover, the second assumption does not seem to me to be plausible. It would be difficult to show *how* the process of perceiving might have developed from that of sensing. The difficulty would be very much like that of showing how the process of remembering might have developed from perceiving, or from sensing.

(iii) At one time Professor Ayer defended phenomenalism on the ground that "the only alternative to it, once we have

---

[9] Compare the criticism of phenomenalism in Arthur Pap, *Analytische Erkenntnistheorie* (Vienna, 1955), ch. ii.

agreed to the use of the sense-datum terminology is the iron-curtain theory of perception: that physical objects are there sure enough but we can never get at them, because all we can observe is sense-data: and surely this theory at least can be shown to be untenable." [10] The doubtful step in this argument, I think, is the premise that, once we have adopted the sense-datum terminology, we must say that "all we can observe is sense-data." If Ayer took "observe" to be synonymous with "perceive," then his argument was an instance of what, in Chapter Ten, we called the sense-datum fallacy. And in this case, the statement "All we can observe is sense-data" is false. But if he took "observe" to be synonymous with "sense" (as we have been using "sense" and as he used it in *The Foundations of Empirical Knowledge*), then, although it is now true to say that all one can observe—all one can *sense*—is sense-data, this statement no longer implies that, if phenomenalism is false, one "can never get at" physical objects. For we may now say, what might have been less appropriate at the beginning of this book, that one *can* get at them—in the only relevant sense of this expression—by *perceiving* them.

---

[10] A. J. Ayer, *Philosophical Essays* (London, 1954), p. 143.

Index

Index

Brentano, Franz, 8, 168-170, 181, 185
Broad, C. D., 31, 44, 154
Burks, Arthur W., 164
Butler, Bishop, 29

Carnap, Rudolf, 10, 22, 23, 26, 29, 108, 175-177
Certainty, 19-21, 63-65
  "certain" defined, 19
  probability and certainty, 25
Chastaing, M., 65
Chatalian, George, 193
Chwistek, Leon, 103
Clifford, W. K., 9, 11, 100
Coffey, P., 103, 152
"Common sensible," 83, 132
Confirmation, see Probability
Copi, Irving, 8
Criteria, 30-39
  of evidence, see Evidence, marks of
  of rightness, 31
"Critical Realism," 157-158

Democritus, 127-128
Demonstrative terms, 163-164
Descartes, René, 32-33, 36, 154
Drake, Durant, 157
"Dubitable," 11, 12-13
Ducasse, C. J., 35, 79, 117, 129, 139
Duggan, Timothy, 88
Duncan-Jones, Austin, 31, 99

Edel, Abraham, 8
Edwards, Paul, 21
Emotions, see Feelings
"Emotive theory of evidence," 104-112
Empirical criterion of evidence, see Empiricism, as an epistemic thesis
Empiricism:
  as an epistemic thesis, 66, 67-95, 101, 195-196

as a genetic thesis, 49-50, 52, 70, 133-137, 196
Ethics, 96-112, 139-141
  see also Right
Evidence:
  "adequate evidence" defined, 5
  "emotive theory of evidence," 104-112
  "evidence-bearing" characteristics, see next entry
  marks of evidence, 32-35, 67-95, 100-101
  "objective evidence," 87
  requirement of total evidence, 26, 28, 85
Expecting, 181-185

Farber, Marvin, 119
Feelings, 104-109, 123, 137, 141
Feigl, Herbert, 100, 171, 174
Fichte, J. G., 134
Findlay, J. N., 109
Firth, Roderick, 57, 160, 193, 194
Flew, Antony, 17, 18, 21, 23, 120
Frege, Gottlob, 108, 171
Furlong, E. J., 94, 111

Geach, Peter, 171
"Given," 53
Goodman, Nelson, 25, 155

Halldén, Sören, 139
Hallucination, 61, 82, 122, 162-164
  "veridical hallucination," 157
Hare, R. M., 31, 140
Hartland-Swann, John, 15
Hawkins, D. J. B., 128, 159
Hegel, G. W. F., 64
Hempel, C. G., 23, 36
Hobbes, Thomas, 34
Holland, R. F., 94
Holt, E. B., 130
Hospers, John, 32, 104, 174-175
Hudson, H., 155
Hume, David, 74-75, 101, 145-146

Index

Index

Prichard, H. A., 7, 32, 90, 104, 118, 146, 151-152, 156-157
Primary qualities, 126-127, 130-133
Probability, 22-29, 56, 95
    "emotive theory" of, 109
    as a "guide of life," 24-27
    inductive sense, 23-27
    probability and certainty, 25, 65-66
    probability and empiricism, 68-69, 71-74
    statistical sense, 27
"Proper objects of sense," 83-84
"Psychologism," 107-109

Quine, W. V., 164
Quinton, A. M., 44, 57, 62

Realism, see "New Realism" and "Critical Realism"
Reichenbach, Hans, 180-181
Reid, Thomas, 75, 83-84, 117, 129, 159, 160, 161, 162, 163
Remembering, 86, 90-94, 110-111
Richards, I. A., 185
Right:
    absolute and practical senses, 7, 14, 37, 88
    "right-making" characteristics, 30-32, 97
Ross, W. D., 7
Russell, Bertrand, 7, 26, 29, 61, 100, 102, 103, 133
Ryle, Gilbert, 18, 48, 91, 117, 152, 166

Schilpp, P. A., 102, 121
Schlick, Moritz, 19-20, 62, 174-175
Schopenhauer, Arthur, 161
Scriven, Michael, 174
Secondary qualities, 126-141
Sellars, R. W., 152, 157-158
Sellars, W. S., 32, 100, 104, 171, 174
"Sense-data," 121-123

see also Appearances *and* Appear words
"Sense-datum fallacy," 151-153, 158, 197
Sensible characteristics, 83-85, 126
Sensing, 115-125
    see also Appear words
Sextus Empiricus, 11, 32, 47
Sibley, F. N., 166
Sidgwick, Henry, 98
"Sign behavior," 177-180
Skepticism, 74, 100-103, 195-196
Smythies, J. R., 167
"Specific response," 181
Steenberghen, Fernand von, 87
Stevenson, C. L., 100
Stimulus, proper, 144-149, 162-164
Stimulus object, 145
Stout, G. F., 117
Strong, C. A., 158
"Substitute stimulus," 178-180
Surprise:
    as a mark of believing, 182-183
    as a mark of evidence, 36-37
Synthetic *a priori*, 105, 112

Taine, Hippolyte, 157
Taking, 56, 76-80, 82, 87
    defined, 77
    "sensible taking," 84-90, 87, 111
Taylor, Richard, 184
Testing, contrasted with justifying, 54
Thomas, St., 102
Titchener, E. B., 161
Toulmin, Stephen, 22-23, 54, 109
"True," 6, 8, 16, 19, 38, 105-112, 140

"Unreasonable," definition of, 5
Urmson, J. O., 17, 22
Use of words, 175

Venn, John, 36
Vesey, G. N. A., 165

Index